LifeSpan

The author taking an editorial conference at *Vogue*, 1943
(*photograph by Norman Parkinson*)

Audrey Withers

LifeSpan

An Autobiography

Peter Owen
London & Chester Springs PA

PETER OWEN PUBLISHERS
73 Kenway Road London SW5 0RE
Peter Owen books are distributed in the USA by
Dufour Editions Inc. Chester Springs PA 19425–0449

First published in Great Britain 1994
© Audrey Kennett 1994

ISBN 0–7206–0927–5

A catalogue record for this book is available from
the British Library

Printed and made by Cromwell Press Melksham

Contents

Souldern Pond and the Hanging Garden seen
from the window of Souldern Court
(*woodcut by Paul Nash, 1929*)

*

Illustrations are on pp. 97–104
The photograph of the author on p. 97 is reproduced by courtesy
of Lord Snowdon. All other photographs are from the author's
collection.
The woodcut above, the watercolour drawing on p. 101 and the
drawings on pp. 102–4 are reproduced by kind permission of the
Principal and Fellows of Somerville College, Oxford.

Prologue

I am conscious of having led a very privileged life, not only in a personal and professional sense, but because of my early experience of the world as it was in previous generations. Later on, I enjoyed the benefits brought by cars and air travel, without which I could not have seen and enjoyed so much. No doubt technology and engineering will develop to an unimaginable degree. The clock can go forward, but it cannot go back. An industrial estate cannot become open country again; a motorway cannot revert to a quiet lane; the sky above an airport cannot hold only those silent watchers, sun, moon and stars. It is my consciousness of privilege that has prompted me to outline my long life.

I have also had the good fortune to live in beautiful places, from the Lake District and the Cotswolds in childhood, to school in St Andrews, college at Oxford, home in Oxfordshire villages and an Essex farmhouse. All my working life has been in London which, although not beautiful, in the sense that Paris, Prague and St Petersburg are beautiful, is perhaps the most interesting city in the world, with hidden treasures to be discovered throughout a lifetime, and unparalleled offerings in museums and galleries, concerts and theatres.

I have been able to widen the span of my own experience by drawing upon those of my father and my husband. My father had a wide circle of friends among the poets and artists of the period between the two world wars; and I quote from their correspondence and describe them as guests in my parents' homes.

Some lives have a certain continuity: the same sort of work; the same home, and a family growing up in it; a lasting circle of friends. My life has been sliced into sections which vary so much that they might be separate incarnations. And just as different muscles are developed by different sports, so the varying demands made by changes in work and in marriage call certain elements into play, leaving others unused. My life has moved from remote country to Central London, from the fashion world to farming. I have, for thirty years, been deeply involved with the former Soviet Union. I have had two husbands who were at opposite poles in every conceivable way. Now that I am alone I have the curious but rather restful sensation of being myself: my whole self and nothing but myself. Successful partners fit themselves together – which means toning down, if not suppressing, some tendencies or tastes that are felt to be inappropriate. Alone, one can do and say precisely what one pleases, without prior thought or consultation. Perhaps this single life sounds self-centred, but it need not be. It is just that, in everything one does, the decision is entirely one's own.

As, basically, we owe everything to our parents, and as my parents were remarkable people, who grew up in the reign of Victoria and lived through the Second World War, I shall start with their lives, which began in the far-off 1870s.

1

My mother, Mary Summers, was born in 1870, the last of eleven children, two of whom died in childhood. Her mother died soon after giving birth to her, worn out by child-bearing – like so many women before the arrival of contraception. Her father died when she was six, leaving not only her but some of her seven brothers orphans before they reached their teens. I have often wondered if it was this experience that brought about a characteristic they all shared: a marked inability to give expression to their emotions, which in turn created a barrier to the expression of emotions by others. My mother talked freely about everyday affairs, but when deeper matters arose she was at a loss for words – and this was an embarrassment to me also.

Her only sister married young, and her sister's children made my mother an aunt at the age of five. Unfortunately she was taken to live with this sister, who was described later by one of her brothers as 'a stern hard character; the milk of human kindness had no place in her anatomy. She worshipped money'. She had married one of two wealthy brothers who had made the extraordinary pact that only one of them would marry, in order to keep the money in one family. She was the dominant personality in the marriage, and this led to a strange sequel. She died in her forties and, released from her firm hand, her husband and sons gambled away their fortune and drank themselves to death.

But my mother's young life had some bright spots. When she was still in her early teens one of her brothers would carry her off to Switzerland, France or Germany; and an elder brother who had been up at Oxford insisted that my mother should go there also: to Somerville, founded only a few years earlier. She always cherished the memory of her college days, and made a lifelong friend of one of her contemporaries, Cornelia Sorabji, India's first woman barrister, who became my godmother.

The background of my father, Percy Withers, was very different. He seldom talked about his early days, and I know only that he was the youngest of four boys and that his mother died when he was eleven. His father was a clerk, on low pay; he died just as my father was leaving school. There was no money, and his only prospect was to become a shop assistant. However, to his eternal gratitude, the two eldest brothers came to his rescue. Though only recently themselves graduated as doctors, they financed him as a medical student at Owens College, forerunner of Manchester University. My father's tastes developed fast; he read widely, wrote poetry and did an occasional book review. He also got his medical degree, set up a practice in Hale, and married my mother.

In those days to 'set up a practice' was a risky and lonely undertaking. You put a brass plate on your door and waited for patients, who might or might not turn up. A doctor's entire income came from his patients, and doctors' bills, like others, could be paid promptly, belatedly or not at all. It was lonely, because there was no such thing as a group practice. A doctor could be called upon by a patient on any day of the week, at any hour of the day or night. My father's health was not robust, and he began to dread a ring of the doorbell in the early hours and the loss of sleep it would bring.

To set against such problems, the doctors of those days had rich personal rewards. They occupied a special place in the community; they were held in respect and even affection. They became the intimate friends of families, entrusted with secrets unknown to others, and so were better able to handle those situations in which mental and emotional factors were bound up with the purely physical ailments which are all that doctors see today. They were holistic before their time.

My sister Monica was born in 1900, and I came five years later. When I was only about a year old my father contracted double pneumonia – a deadly illness, at that time usually fatal. His doctor brothers rushed to help and he came through alive but very badly affected. The situation was extremely serious. My parents were not penniless, because my mother had been allotted Preference shares in the family steel company, John Summers and Sons, a very successful company with an interesting history. My mother's father began as a 'clogger' – making the clogs that were universally worn by working people in Lancashire. At the Great Exhibition of 1851 he bought a machine for making the nails that fastened leather tops to wooden soles. One of his younger sons – brilliant in business as well as engineering – took over the management and created a large steel manufacturing company, employing the greater part of the population of Shotton. After the last war it suffered the trauma of being nationalized, denationalized and renationalized, and finally it closed down.

One winter day my mother's two eldest brothers came to tea. As usual, the conversation was small talk; they expressed their sympathy, but that was all. She saw them out and, as she returned, noticed in the dim gaslight an envelope on the hall table. It contained a cheque which kept them for the rest of their lives, and enabled them to give their children many privileges. Shortly after this my father sold his practice and the family moved away.

We went to Abbot's Bay, which had been built as a holiday cottage on a promontory into Derwentwater. This was the first home I knew, and it was bliss. Now that the Lake District is invaded by tourists it is difficult to imagine the peace and freedom of the lives we led. The only other building in sight was a cottage where we got our milk. We could get bread and basic groceries from Grange-in-Borrowdale, two miles away. Everything else had to come from Keswick, eight miles by bicycle along a rough mountain road, or three miles by rowing-boat, impossible to use in storms. For servants they had a married couple. They also employed a governess, and often there were visitors, so huge quantities of food had to be transported. All the water was pumped by hand, and all the wood for our fires (we used no coal) had to be sawn up and the logs split.

The Abbot's Bay promontory was between two areas of woodland called Brandlehow and Manesty. The National Trust had been set up only a few years earlier. Its first properties were in the Lake District and included these two woods. My parents held certain beliefs long before these acquired the status of names. They were premature Greens, environmentally conscious, World Wildlifers, so it was natural that my father should take on the guardianship of these woods on behalf of the National Trust. Every walk we took went through them, and all the year round we collected dead wood from which my father built the huge bonfire that was lit on Guy Fawkes' night, with an effigy of the Guy, in a highly flammable oilskin coat, perched on top. From all round the lake people came by boat to see the sight and to join in the fun. There were fireworks too. It was a great event.

The wildlife of the area was totally undisturbed. Red squirrels abounded and nesting-boxes for birds were attached to the Scotch firs. One day I was in the woods with my father when he was searching for an owls' nest. At the age of five I was restricted to searching near the ground, and put my head down between two halves of a tree-trunk that had fallen, broken and rotted. Out in my face flew a grey owl, and, deep in the trunk, were four bright yellow eyes, embedded in grey fluff.

Every day before breakfast my father swam in the lake, even throughout the winter, when he had to break the ice. He did it for pure enjoyment, and in later years, when there was no longer a lake, he took cold baths instead. But of course at Abbot's Bay the lake was our neighbourhood and our playground. We were taught to swim at an early age. The lake was at our feet, and behind us were the hills and the mountains. The nearest hill was Catbells – home, we believed, of Mrs Tiggywinkle. It was also the nearest place for picking bilberries, which make the most delicious of all fruit pies. Further away, and higher, was Causey Pike, which Monica and I had each passed the endurance test of climbing on our fifth birthday.

The connection with the National Trust brought some of its founder members to Abbot's Bay to visit their woodland properties; and when my parents moved south, my father served on its Governing Council for many years. For in 1912 my parents decided that we must leave Abbot's Bay. My brother, christened

Michael Derwent as a sign of my father's passionate love for the district, was born in 1910. My sister Monica needed a fuller education than a governess could give. I expect my mother was feeling the strain of bringing up a family in such a distant place. The decision was heart-breaking for my father, and indeed I doubt that he ever quite got over it. He suffered the same sense of loss as in parting from someone you deeply love. It was strange that a man who had spent his whole life in towns should have had such a profound need for uninhabited countryside, the wilder the better. He needed to live quite dangerously – deliberately taking a rowing-boat out in storms, and walking alone on the fells in the worst of gales, fog and snow. His consolation was to write two books about his beloved Lake District: *In a Cumberland Dale* and *Friends in Solitude*.

We moved to Broadway, Worcestershire. I believe it is now an overrun tourist attraction, but even then it was an unusual village in that it had attracted a small colony of actors, singers and artists, lured by the presence of one of the most famous actresses of her day – the American, Mary Anderson. My father was enraptured to have her as a neighbour, since as a young man he had been among the crowd that gathered at the Manchester railway station where she was due to arrive, and had queued for a gallery seat to see her in her famous double role as Hermione and Perdita in *The Winter's Tale*. She and her husband, Antonio de Navarro, lived in one of the most beautiful houses in Broadway. In later years, when they and my parents were in Cambridge, A.E. Housman wrote to my father: 'I will walk with you to the Navarros' door. I shall not cross the threshold myself; but I am not going to keep you out of Paradise.'

Of course, in such a small community, newcomers were visited and quickly absorbed. The Navarros became friends, and one day it came out that we loved to swim, and missed our lake. We were made welcome to swim in the Navarros' pool, and way before they were up, my father, Monica and I would cycle up the long hill that runs through the village, take our swim, and freewheel all the way back for breakfast.

Our own home, Kilsant House, was in Cotswold stone; three storeys and an attic. Virginia creeper and wisteria grew up the walls, and some former owner had hopefully planted a vine. But the grapes never ripened. Monica and I liked nothing better than to climb anything in sight, and the stone-tiled roof, with its gullies and gables, was a favourite playground. One day we decided that Michael, aged two, should not be left out of our adventure, so we hauled him on to the roof, sat him comfortably with his feet against a chimney-pot and continued our climb. Our mother came out, and it was only much later that I realized how remarkable it was that she did not shout or scream but called quietly, 'Will you bring Michael down, please? I want to give him a bath.'

We were very fortunate to have had parents who never showed – and I think never felt – alarm at anything we did. We used literally to run along the top of a ten-foot garden wall, and it never occurred to anyone that we might fall off. We climbed trees, and one day I did fall off and hurt my shoulder. The next day, on our morning bathe, I used only my other arm, until my father told me not to be silly. When later I remarked that my shoulder made funny noises I was taken to have an X-ray, which showed a cracked bone. The same freedom applied, even more importantly, to books. My father had a large library and we had the run of it, so I was very surprised when, arriving at boarding-school with *Adam Bede* as my book for the train, it was taken away and given back only when I went home for the holidays. I suppose it was the episode of the girl having a baby under a hedge which shook them: but I had taken that in my stride, as children do.

Nowadays, when slimming diets are a constant topic, I remember the meals grown-ups ate in my childhood, and find it astonishing that no one seemed to put on weight. My father was over six feet tall and very lean; my mother was medium height and far from plump; yet this was their daily diet. Breakfast: bacon and eggs, or kidneys, or fish, or kedgeree, set out on a copper stand heated by oil lamps; beside it, a ham or cold roast pheasant or partridge, when they were in season. Lunch was a two-course meal: meat with two vegetables, and a pudding or pie. My parents were both of North Country origin and 'tea' to them meant scones, buns and cakes large and small, with bread and butter and jam thrown in. Dinner was three courses, starting with soup. Sunday lunch was special: almost always a huge roast sirloin, followed by a fruit tart, made with plums (bottled for out-of-season use) or apples stored in the barn, or raspberries and red currants, or gooseberries, which my mother insisted on picking before they were fully ripe – 'fair murder' the gardener called it. Preparations for Christmas began in autumn, when the mixture for about ten huge plum puddings was prepared, ready for each birthday throughout the year. All the ingredients were sliced by hand, bottles of brandy were poured in and there was a liberal sprinkling of silver threepenny bits and pseudo-silver trinkets. Finally, every member of the family and the household had to stir the mixture.

Everything was as time-consuming (and human-energy con-suming) as it could be. Since the only running water was in the single bathroom, every bedroom had a basin, and a maid brought a can of hot water to wash in. These cans were brass, and of course brass needs to be polished. The main rooms were lit by oil lamps, which meant that wicks had to be changed, lamps cleaned and filled. Everyone went to bed with a candle, and though the candlesticks – also of brass – had wide bases, my mother could often be seen kneeling on the stair carpet with a hot iron in one hand and newspaper in the other, to suck up the candle-grease. Buckets and cooking pans were made of iron, and were correspondingly heavy. Carpet sweepers were the nearest thing to vacuum cleaners. The washing of clothes and household linen involved a mangle from which the water poured before things were pegged to a washing-line to dry; and heavy irons were heated on the stove, to be tested by touching them with a licked finger. Spring-cleaning was scrupulously carried out. My mother herself dusted every one of the 3,000-odd books in my father's library, and polished the shelves before putting them back.

I don't know how it started, but my family always loved to dress up. Trunks in the attic were full of costumes from various countries and periods, as well as a mixture of odds and ends which could have been anything except normal clothing. We wore fancy dress for every birthday, for Christmas, and indeed whenever we found an excuse to do so. Our costume wardrobe was large enough, in every sense, to be able to fit out our visitors as well. At Christmas a church choir would drop in to sing, and also a group of handbell-ringers. They were invited into the drawing-room to be given a glass of wine and a piece of cake; and their astonishment at being welcomed by a gentleman wearing a wig, brocade waistcoat and satin breeches – my father's favourite costume – changed to amusement as they recognized us, one by one.

Life in the English countryside was little changed from what it had been in the previous century. Cars were a rarity. When an invalid aunt came to stay, a pony and cart were hired for expeditions, and I travelled in the cart with her instead of on the back of my father's bicycle. When we helped with haymaking, everything was done with scythes, rakes and forks. Horses drew the haywains, and the farmhands rose high in the air as they built up the haystack under their feet, to be finally finished by the thatchers. In the spring there were miles of orchards in the Cotswold valleys and spreading up the hills: cherry, plum, apple and pear – large trees under which you could walk. The air was full of their scent and the hum of bees. Wild flowers were in abundance; in spring the coppices were full of bluebells, primroses and wood anemones; fields were yellow with cowslips. Even though unusually sophisticated in its residents, the village management remained as of old. A member of the fire brigade visited my parents to tell them that, in case of fire, an hour's warning must be given, because the horses that drew the engine were grazing on the hillside and had to be caught.

My father had literary friends who came to stay, but a writer of a different calibre, nearer home, was Marie Corelli, whose novels – with those of Ethel M. Dell – met the perennial demand for sensation, which could then be satisfied only by the printed word. Her special hype was religion which, mixed with sex, was a potent cocktail. She lived in Stratford-upon-Avon and possessed a houseboat in which she took guests on the river. She invited my father – but not my mother – on one of these cruises. He didn't accept. One winter afternoon my parents returned home to be told that a lady had called, who preferred to sit in the hall. In the dim light there didn't seem to be anyone about except the Irish wolfhound; but then, in a corner beyond him, they saw a small crouching figure. Marcus, a large but friendly dog, had gone up to investigate the visitor. She had panicked and he had decided to mount guard until my parents took over. I think this was the end of what had never been a beautiful friendship.

One 'of the reasons for our leaving the Lake District was Monica's need for better education; and the Cotswolds were chosen as being near Cheltenham, with its celebrated girls' boarding-school. But for some reason our parents turned against it, and after a year or two of governesses Monica was sent to a school in Woking. When war broke out in 1914 my father felt he must help in any way he could, and offered his services as a doctor. He was put in charge of a convalescent home for war wounded at Standish, near Gloucester. My mother and Michael went with him, and I was dispatched to join Monica at boarding-school.

It is impossible to explain how intelligent parents could possibly have consigned their children to such an archaic school, Dickensian in everything except ill-treatment. There must have been about twenty-five pupils, aged from ten to seventeen. The staff 'lived in', and their rooms were named after appropriate virtues. Of the two headmistresses, one was labelled 'Justice' and the other 'Mercy'. The French teacher lived in 'Patriotism'. 'Justice' was intimidating from the fact that she wore spectacles so thick that her eyes were hugely enlarged. Also, she was the one who, after morning prayers, went out into the hall to beat the gong for breakfast, and anyone who had broken a rule (of which there were many) had to step out of line and confess – at the top of one's voice, to make it heard over the noise of the gong. History consisted of a textbook ruled out in columns: the king or queen, dates of their reign, wars, events such as the Black Death, leading politicians, writers. Half a page had to be learnt at a time and recited in class.

In the holidays we went to the Standish Hospital, where we slept in a tent in the grounds because there was no room indoors. The soldiers were all Australian and Canadian, and some had come from such distant backwoods that they had never seen a city. When a new patient arrived, a form had to be filled in,

17

giving all manner of details, one of which was the name of the Expeditionary Force. In one case, thinking he knew it, my father queried, 'Mesopotamia?' 'Oh no, sir,' said a shocked voice, 'Church of England' – which my father felt reflected rather nicely on the strangely named religious cults that were springing up.

While at Standish, my father got to know William Rothenstein, who had a country cottage nearby and was working on a group portrait commissioned by a Cambridge college. He needed a model, so dressed up my father in full academic regalia and arranged him in the correct pose, so that all that Rothenstein needed to do later would be to set the real professor's head on the model's shoulders. Among Rothenstein's visitors was Max Beerbohm, who did a fine cartoon drawing of my father – then in his forties – which he grew precisely to resemble, twenty years later. Caricaturists are often savage, but Max, though penetrating, was never unkind. Someone who knew him well could remember only one cruel comment, made in a conversation about Aubrey Beardsley: 'Even his lungs were diseased.'

Of course I was only a child at that time but, years later, I attended Max Beerbohm's opening of an exhibition in a Bond Street gallery. There Beerbohm described an incident in his early life. He had gone to Paris to see Rodin, from whom he needed an introduction, and decided to catch him at an exhibition he was opening. Max arrived too late for the actual moment, but introduced himself to Rodin, who pulled a piece of paper out of his pocket to write down the address. Later, Max realized that there was writing on the other side of the sheet, and turned it over to find the entire text of Rodin's opening speech. It read: 'Mesdames et Messieurs, l'exposition est ouverte.'

My parents made good friends with the nurses at the hospital, and two of them, sisters in their twenties, talked about schools and praised the one they had been to – St Leonards, in St Andrews, Fife. Our parents were impressed, and we were duly taken from Woking and dispatched to St Andrews. Monica, already sixteen, went to the senior school and I to the junior. When I thought about it in later years I felt that Monica had had a very raw deal. Before she went to school we had been educated together, though I was considerably younger. She had wasted years at that travesty of a school in Woking, and then had only two years left for true education. All the more honour to her that she went on to make a distinguished career as a teacher, headmistress and inspector of schools.

2

St Leonards was among the first public schools for girls. It consisted of about eight houses, dotted over a large area, a central school building and extensive playing-fields, high above the harbour, right on the sea front; and every so often the local sea fog – the haar – swept in so thickly, you could not see the nearest player. Over it all loomed the impressive towers of the ancient ruined abbey. Our swimming-pool was formed by a breakwater between two lines of rock. Twice a day the cold North Sea tide swept over it, and the temperature was sometimes in the mid-fifties. The unheated bedrooms were so cold that, in winter, we used to put our clothes on top of the blankets: we would have gone to bed in them if we had been allowed to. Wartime rationing had encouraged the school to lay down barrels of oversalted herrings, and we spread a mixture of margarine and mashed potato on our bread. It was a Spartan life, and some girls did not have the physique to stand it. I just got chilblains.

Scottish education has always been admired, and rightly so. The Scots have shared with European countries a high respect for education and for teachers: a prerequisite for attracting talented people into the profession. We were fortunate to have teachers whose enthusiasm for their subjects spilled over on to us. They were sometimes remarkably unconventional. Our English teacher decided that the best way for getting us into Paradise Lost was to allot us parts in the conference Satan held on being thrown out of heaven. I was Beelzebub, and was reading my speech when a government inspector walked in. Far from calling off the performance, we were told to carry on: a new experience for the inspector. The scripture teacher might herself have been an Old Testament prophet when she read parts of the Book of Isaiah.

Few children have the awareness to adapt their character, built up at home, into one that is suitable for school. I was unpopular because I continued to do what I was encouraged to do at home – to express my own opinions, which were not always those held by others. The young are extremely conventional among themselves, however unconventional they may seem to an older generation. I was often in breach of those conventions, and regarded as 'stuck up' and 'always wanting to be different'. I expect I was insufferable. I was also unhappy.

Like many adolescents I went through a bad time in my mid-teens. As in all boarding-schools of the period, religion played an important part, and it was assumed that girls in their teens would be confirmed – which I found deeply disturbing. There was only one person I could talk to – Mrs Robertson, who knew relatives of ours and lived near the school. Our acquaintance soon became a close relationship. She kept her front door unlocked, and I can still feel the overwhelming sense of peace and security when I stood in the quiet hall, the rumble of the cobbled street shut out, and heard her soft Scots voice call, 'Come away, dearie.' Nothing that I said upset or even surprised her. She never admonished or advised me; she simply listened and, I felt, loved me. She was the older generation friend whom every adolescent needs. Eventually I was confirmed – from exhaustion rather than conviction. But I never took communion after I left school. My mother went to early service alone, but made no comment, let alone reproach. After I left school I wrote to Mrs Robertson to thank her for what she had done for me. She replied that my letter had given her great happiness, and asked me to remember, all my life, to do the same for others. I hope I have carried out her wish. I never saw her again. She died during my first term at college.

I went back only once to my old school, the year after I left, while I still had friends there. (I have never been one for visiting the past; things have always changed and memories are spoilt.) I got my entrance to Somerville with the intention of reading English, then had second thoughts. A new subject had been invented, pretentiously called Modern Greats but later, more accurately, PPE (Philosophy, Politics and Economics). It seemed to me that I could go on reading literature all my life but could never tackle such abstruse subjects alone. My change of plan had been accepted, as I rather proudly told one of the mistresses at school. However, she threw a bucket of cold water over me, saying, 'I hope you've done the right thing. I think you have to be clever to tackle Modern Greats.'

As I came back from Scotland after that visit, on a cloudless summer day, the train passed through one northern industrial town after another and, in each case, the sun was blotted out from miles before we reached the town until we had left it far behind. I don't believe the inhabitants ever saw the sun. By the mid-thirties much was done to limit the discharge from factory chimneys; but when the 1939 war brought bombing raids, restrictions were lifted, since smoke-screens were the best protection, and it was not until the late fifties that they were reimposed. I can pinpoint the event which caused that action to be taken. London had been having a series of Dickensian fogs in winter months. Flares were lit round the Marble Arch and Hyde Park Corner circuits, traffic crawled. In one December fog, when the Smithfield Agricultural Show was being held, cattle died from breathing the polluted air. People had been dying from the same cause for years, but to lose prize bulls was too much.

To return to the 1914–18 war: my father was moved from the Standish home to the main hospital in Cambridge, but he went down again with double pneumonia, and was so weakened that he was unfit to take up the hospital appointment. Instead, he was made vice-chairman of the Recruiting Board. It was 1917; they were scraping the bottom of the barrel. Recruits were categorized as A, B or C, with three grades for each letter. Already it was being said that Britain had a C3 population. My father hated every minute of it. He was appalled at the sickly specimens paraded in front of them, whom they were under great pressure to pass into service. He described it as 'the most desolating and the most degrading task I was ever set to do'.

The bright side of his life in Cambridge was his association with the university, which was a shadow of its usual self. Young dons had been called up; the only students were those who had been rejected for military service. There were many vacant places at high tables and he was often invited to fill one. He was a great success – principally for one reason. It was high table convention to avoid all topics that were the province of anyone present: which meant practically anything of interest. My father could start a conversation on any subject; conventions meant nothing to him, and the result was that dons were enjoying dinners at which opinions were knocked to and fro like tennis-balls. One professor told my mother, 'Your husband ought to be paid a salary just to come and dine.'

When I went up to Oxford I was the only newcomer who knew how to punt, so I was in demand for giving instruction. Oxford and Cambridge have many things in common but give them different names and do them in different ways. For instance, they punt from opposite ends of the boat. I did not dare to say it at the time, but I thought the Cambridge way of standing on the raised platform was the proper choice.

When the war ended my parents returned to Broadway. Our lives were transformed by the gift of a car from an uncle who greatly admired Henry Ford and gave my mother the original Tin Lizzie. It was an amazing car, with just two pedals – accelerator and brake. Its secret weapon was the petrol tank. The dial would show what looked like sufficient petrol; and we were slow to realize that, going uphill, it might not reach the engine. An aunt came to stay with us. At home she possessed a very grand limousine and her former coachman had become her chauffeur. We took her for a drive, with my father at the wheel, and our car duly played its trump card when going up a long steep hill. To my aunt's dismay and astonishment we all jumped out and began to walk up it, while my father reversed and drove up the hill backwards, bumping into the banks on either side. He was not a good driver.

Our house in Broadway was rented. Now the landlord wanted to sell it but my parents did not want to buy it, so they house-hunted for months. After the war, with hundreds of thousands of people remaking their lives, houses were snapped up. One day in 1920 they arrived in an Oxfordshire village, eight miles from Banbury, and bought Souldern Court. It is the home I remember best. I was growing up and, when I went up to Oxford, it was near enough for me to bring college friends over for the day. Also it was the house visited by the writers and artists who were my father's closest friends and from whose correspondence I shall quote later.

Souldern was a small, remote village that did not have, like Broadway, a social life of its own. The lady of the manor, a widow, called on my mother, who inquired about the village people, always her chief interest. She got the unpromising reply that they all had more than they deserved. Experience revealed that her gardener's wife was her drudge, expected to scrub floors until days before her children were born, with the result that they were physically stunted and mentally retarded. A group of old people lived in almshouses and were delighted when my father dropped in and chatted to them about their ailments. One of them suffered from 'this 'ere bumboodle in the back'. The men had all been farmworkers, miserably paid. Some of them had never been as far as Banbury. Radios were unknown; there was no electricity and no public transport. Education was minimal, so people read with difficulty and had few books, and no magazines or newspapers. In the winter they would go to bed when it grew dark, to save fuel and keep warm. From birth to death it was a life of deprivation.

My mother was both imaginative and practical in her relations with neighbours in need, utterly remote from a Lady Bountiful. A van drove into the village once a week, selling household necessities such as Sunlight soap. The village women could afford to buy only one piece at a time – and it was soft, melting away quickly. My mother bought a quantity and put it in the airing cupboard, where it hardened. She told her friends among the village women that, if they liked, she would sell them her hardened soap; and they liked that very much. During the General Strike of 1926 no coal was delivered. The villagers could afford only a hundredweight at a time and soon ran out, while my parents bought it by the truckload, tipped into the cellar. So they weighed up hundredweights of their coal, filled packing-cases, loaded a trolley and pushed it round the village, selling each load for the lower price they themselves had paid for it, in bulk. Though well into middle age, they asked for no help, even from the gardener.

One thing my mother never did was to read. It was quite extraordinary, and my father could not get over it. When my sister and I were little and loved to be read to, she would fall asleep at vital moments of the story and we had to shake her and cry out 'What happens next?' Another curious thing was that she knew very well how to provide the food for meals and how they ought to be served, but she never cooked anything herself. Servants had the day off on a bank holiday, but the cook had to prepare a dish which could be heated up for supper, and for lunch we went out for a picnic. Cousins who stayed with us each Easter remembered with an amazed amusement how we would cower behind a hedge on an icy Good Friday, clutching the sandwich wrappings to keep them from blowing away. The result of holding the kitchen at arms' length, as it were, meant that my sister and I left home without ever having boiled an egg.

My father frequently went up to London to attend meetings of the Council of the National Trust and the Council for the Preservation of Ancient Buildings. He also greatly enjoyed his club, the Savile, and the private art galleries, especially the Redfern, whose proprietor had become a friend – from whom I, in turn, bought drawings later. My father had a good eye for drawings; paintings were beyond his budget. I always felt that if he had been in London earlier in the century he would have come away with impressionists and post-impressionists, or whatever was going at the then affordable prices. However, a new field of art came into his life through his friendship with Laurence Binyon, then head of the Far Eastern department of the British Museum. Binyon introduced him to Japanese prints. My father gave a number to the Walker Art Gallery in Manchester and later I had the pleasure of seeing these in their pristine brilliance, because – unlike those that I inherited, which I hung on my walls and have endlessly enjoyed – they were kept in portfolios, away from light. My father had always kept them in the same way; as also his collection of etchings and woodcuts.

Laurence Binyon was a charming and immensely talented man. Though a specialist in Far Eastern art, he had a wide knowledge of European art, and was of course also a poet. He knew enough Japanese to be able to translate the calligraphy that ornaments their prints, and his knowledge of Italian enabled him to make a translation of Dante. I remember his telling a story which illustrates that strange scenario in which a man prepared to spend hundreds of pounds on one thing cannot bring himself to spend a few pence on another. A rich art collector invited the Binyons to tea. His flat was up several flights of stairs and two panting delivery men arrived with his latest purchase. Their host realized that they needed to be given something for their pains. His eye fell on a bag of buns (the Binyons' tea), and he gave it to the men.

One of our guests at Souldern was Trenchard Cox – later to become director of the V & A, but then a shy, budding young art historian. We were riveted by his account of a visit to the country house of Sir Philip Sassoon, a patron of the arts. Young Mr Cox found the wealth and formality of his surroundings overpowering; the only touch of real life was an earwig in his gold-tapped bath. At dinner on the first night he was presented with a huge iced *bombe* by one of the posse of footmen. As his trembling hand cut into it, it sailed off its silver platter and landed on an obviously priceless piece of embroidery. This in itself was sufficiently horrifying; but worse still was the fact that everyone was too 'well-bred' to make the slightest comment. An identical *bombe* was produced. The footmen didn't touch the first one, it was simply left to melt. Trenchard Cox was so unnerved that, after a sleepless night, he made his escape early the next morning.

We had a real live Mrs Malaprop in the village: the spinster daughter of a former Dean of Manchester. One December she called on my mother to discuss costumes for the Nativity play at the village school. 'Angels are easy,' said Miss Maclure. 'All it needs are some sheets and safety-pins.' She saw my mother's doubtful expression and said, 'Oh, Mrs Withers, you're always so septic.' When she fell seriously ill my father visited her and asked if there had been a diagnosis. 'Not yet,' she said. 'If only they would make a post-mortem examination I feel sure they would know what is wrong.'

Artists came to Souldern, too. Our close friend from Broadway days, F. L. Griggs, designed a second storey to a small building that housed the electricity-generating engine, as a result of which we climbed a stone stairway to a summerhouse overlooking the garden. Immediately below was a stretch of grass which our gardener always referred to as 'the barn floor': all that remained of what had been a barn was its back wall – but another beautiful barn, its open front supported by stone pillars, still stood there. The barn floor became the stage for a performance of *The Merchant of Venice* by travelling actors intent on bringing the theatre to rural communities. It was fascinating that the unsophisticated audience reacted in much the same way as, I imagine, Shakespeare's original audience did at the Globe Theatre: they hissed the entries of Shylock, played as a villain – as I believe he generally was portrayed. It was on this same piece of grass that Paul Nash chose to stage an imaginary ballet, when he made a drawing in my father's album (of which more later).

Paul Nash was more than a friend, because his watercolour drawings of Souldern established a permanent image of our surroundings. He was an obsessive worker, never without a sketchbook. He made a portrait drawing of me, picking it up day after day while we waited for the gong to announce a meal. I believe it to be almost the only portrait he did of anyone outside his family. The widows of creative men often find consolation in promoting their husbands' work, but this can be overdone. After Paul's death, Margaret Nash set up a small group of 'trustees' and asked me to be one. I was editing *Vogue* at the time, so she thought I was well placed for arranging magazine reproductions. She would call me up and say that an editor wanted to publish a certain drawing – but she wanted him to use another one, and I was to tell him so. It was useless to explain that it was better to let editors have what they wanted unless there were good reasons against it; she thought her own preference was a good enough reason. I was considered uncooperative and dropped. Much as I loved Paul and his work, it was a relief.

In that period between the wars there was a resurgence of the Pre-Raphaelite attitude that art was a part of daily life. Artists were also designers, especially in the fields of textiles and ceramics. 'British designs for British fabrics' was the title of one of our *Vogue* features, showing the work of Duncan Grant, Graham Sutherland, Ben Nicholson and Paul Nash. For many years I had a rug which Paul had designed and which was exhibited at the World Fair at Wembley – chiefly remembered for its statue of the Prince of Wales in butter.

My father was deeply interested in church architecture, especially in its early periods and, above all, Saxon. We visited churches on bicycles for many years, and when we had a car I often drove him. Once, when we were wandering round a village church, the vicar appeared. He gave no greeting but barked at my father, 'Is that your daughter? Then give her your hat.' I told him that I would not walk around the church in my father's trilby but would wait for him outside. It was sad that a clergyman's mind should have been occupied with such trivialities. Now, comparatively few people go into churches either for the services or the architecture, although they would be welcome in any kind of clothing.

As my parents had been members of the National Trust since its earliest days, we naturally visited any houses within our reach that were open to the public. Charlecote Park, an Elizabethan house near Stratford-upon-Avon, had recently come into that category, so we went over to see it. The small group of visitors were taken around by an old servant, and when we reached the Great Hall he addressed us as follows: 'In this very 'all Shakespeare was brought afore the magistrates for shootin' of a deer. 'E oughter 'ave been 'ung. But they let 'im orf, and 'e went up to Lunnon and made a name for 'isself.' Later, at the church, a verger led us up to the tomb of the owner of Charlecote in Shakespeare's time. The parents lay prone, surrounded by the small kneeling figures of their offspring – all, as the verger told us, 'in harleyblaster'.

In the autumn of 1924 I went up to Oxford – to my mother's old college, Somerville. Schooldays are seldom the happiest of one's life, for adolescence is not a happy experience, but college days can deserve that term and came near to doing so for me. It was a thrilling transformation for a girl who, for years, had worn a school uniform, slept in a dormitory and had her days spaced out by the ringing of bells, to have a room of her own and her time to spend as she thought best. The thing that impressed me most was that I was never instructed to do anything; it was entirely my own responsibility. At the beginning of each term my tutor would tell me that various people would be lecturing on various subjects: 'You may like to go.' And never once did she ask whether I had been. In the first week of term lecture halls would be crowded, but only a few remained so. Attendance might drop sharply or steadily; students voted with their feet.

I am convinced that the tutorial system is superior to any other. For an hour each week a student is pitted against someone of superior intellect and knowledge. Points made in the weekly essay must be defended or yielded. There is no one to hide behind; one is out in the open and compelled to draw upon all one's powers. Intellectually, it is the equivalent of a sports training, and equally necessary to get good results.

The PPE school I was reading was in only its second cycle and, since it was so new, there was no clear idea what it was all about. Its life began in the eighteenth century, so I was faced with great tomes to read, from Adam Smith to John Maynard Keynes, plus Descartes, Spinoza, Kant and so on. The sheer volume of it took all the time there was, in term and vacation. My friends in other schools were in the same boat; and I find it hard to understand how today's students can do jobs in the vacations (if there are jobs) and go hiking abroad, whereas we felt the need to study almost all the time, and had reading parties in the long vacation, just to get through the work.

One of these was held in my home in Souldern. My parents went abroad; the servants had holidays; eight of us took over the place. But there was one unwilling participant: our spaniel. My father liked a dog that was an enthusiast for walks. He deplored Bang's habit of hanging behind so that, when he turned to go home, Bang would save himself walking those last few yards. My friends, going out in twos and threes and crying out 'Walk Bang!', made him get up wearily and totter after them. But there was one plus point among all the minuses. My parents ordered bull's-eyes in 7-pound tins. Bang, too, had become addicted. At the sound of the tin being opened he woke from a deep sleep and sat up instantly – and he always got a bull's-eye for his pains. My friends were much taken with this trick, and Bang was ready to oblige every time.

Especially in the summer term I would bring two or three friends over for the day at the weekend, and sometimes we met a visitor who extended an invitation to us in return. A memorable example of this was Emery Walker, an associate of William Morris in the work of the Kelmscott Press. He had a house on the Thames, in Hammersmith, which he filled with friends on Boat Race day. He invited two of us to come. We left Oxford at dawn, because the race was in the morning. Every floor of the tall house was filled, and so was the roof, where we took up our station. As we watched, the boats came into view almost side by side – and suddenly one shot ahead, leaving its rival limping behind. Of course we were baffled and also distressed, because the stricken boat was Oxford's. The tragic answer was that one of the crew had had a heart attack, turning the eight into a helpless seven. But the Boat Race was only the beginning of the day for us. We then proceeded to a matinée of *Saint Joan*, with Sybil Thorndike, and an evening at *The Immortal Hour*, with Gwen Ffrangcon-Davies: the two outstanding theatrical events of the time, and thrilling to us. Luckily my friend's parents had a London flat where we finally fell into bed.

My parents were invited to lunch with Sir Michael Sadler, Master of University College, and they took me with them. He was known by the London galleries as a discerning and compulsive buyer, and his impressive collection overflowed the Master's Lodgings. After lunch he sent me up to the attic to see pictures for which there was no hanging room; they were stacked against one another on the floor. 'And come down by the back stairs,' he said – and with good reason, for Constable watercolours were hung the whole way down. He showed us a glass case full of small, precious objects, and also a sixpenny Bavarian wineglass from Woolworths, saying that it, too, was perfect in its way. Some twenty years later, when I was making the rounds of the galleries myself, and bought an occasional drawing or lithograph, I fell for a Segonzac landscape – and was happy to find that it had been in the Sadler collection.

I had met Robert Bridges and his wife when they were visiting my parents, and they invited me to tea at their house on Boar's Hill. There were several other guests, including Sir Hugh Allen, principal of the Royal College of Music. After tea we went into the garden to play bowls – the Bridges team against the Allen team, and I was in the Bridges'. I had never played bowls and was very nervous, but some angel guided my arm and my shots went nearer the jack than anyone else's. My captain was delighted. 'We've won. You're a genius,' he said.

I encountered Sir Hugh Allen again at a carol-singing in the Sheldonian. The hall was packed, but we weren't making enough noise to satisfy him. We had been singing while sitting down when he exploded, 'It's a disgrace! You aren't doing your best! Everyone who wasn't singing their heart out, stand up!' No one moved. Then up in the highest range of seats a little old man and two old ladies rose bravely but shakily to their feet. Allen looked up at them and said, 'Oh, but you would if you could, wouldn't you?'

It was in the Sheldonian that the Bach Choir held their rehearsals and gave their concerts. For the whole of my first term I sang the Brahms German Requiem with them, and I have never forgotten it. To sing in a choir or play in an orchestra is surely one of the great experiences; one's single feebleness suddenly caught up in a glorious burst of sound. How I got in without an audition I never knew, but, by the second term, they got round to it and I was thrown out.

I had the good fortune to get another kind of education by crossing the Woodstock Road to the Playhouse Theatre opposite. It housed Basil Dean's repertory company which, during my three years at Oxford, put on practically every play by Chekhov, Ibsen, Strindberg, Shaw and others. One could have lived in London during that time and not seen any of them, except by going out to Richmond where Peggy Ashcroft played in the first Chekhov ever, I think, to be performed in England. It had a gifted company, including a very young John Gielgud and his elder brother Val; and I went to every production they put on. It was a wonderful experience for us all but especially for me, living as I was so far from theatres that I had only ever been to a

Manchester pantomime. I have a hazy recollection of the ballet. I was only eight, and can't be sure, but I cling to the belief that I saw Nijinsky and Karsavina in *Le spectre de la rose*.

Ironic verses of the limerick type were circulated. When some branch of philosophy maintained that the external world existed only through man's perception of it, this one appeared:

> There was a young man who said, 'God
> Must find it exceedingly odd
> To think that this tree
> Continues to be
> When there's no one about in the quad.'

To which came a prompt reply from Ronnie Knox, an eminent and witty Roman Catholic:

> Dear Sir, your astonishment's odd.
> I am always about in the quad.
> And that's why the tree
> Continues to be
> Since observed by, yours faithfully, God.

In my time the vice-chancellor was Lord Curzon, former Viceroy of India. A poem was put into his mouth which began, 'My name is George Nathaniel Curzon/I am a very superior person' – and he lived up to this description when a lunch menu for a visit of King George V and Queen Mary was presented to him for his approval. He drew a line through the opening course of soup, pronouncing, 'A gentleman does not eat soup at luncheon.'

Another royal visit caused consternation. This time the King and Queen were to take tea at Christchurch. All its magnificent silver had been spread out for the occasion, and the college notables were waiting to receive their guests when an equerry appeared. He cast an eye over the preparations and said, 'That's fine, but where's the tea-strainer?' As panic broke out – tea-drinkers in earlier times knew of no such thing – the equerry said, 'Don't worry. It's for the Queen. I always carry one with me.' And out of his trouser pocket he pulled a cheap tin tea-strainer and plonked it down among the shining silver.

My first principal of Somerville was Miss Emily Penrose. Her skirts touched the ground so that her feet were invisible, but she moved with such smooth speed that one of my friends insisted that she went on roller skates. She was succeeded by Margery Fry, who came of a family famous for its work in social reform. But while admiring her, I was disappointed at an interview she held with each student who was about to go down. She simply assumed that I should be doing some form of social work, in those days unpaid. When I said that I wanted paid employment, she said my parents could surely afford to keep me. I said that they had been doing so for twenty years and that I wanted to earn my living. The different viewpoints of that conversation showed that even a progressive thinker of one generation can be out of touch with another.

Shortly after graduation I drove my parents up to Yorkshire, where we hoped to witness that rare event in Britain – a total eclipse of the sun. It was due within an hour or so of sunrise on a midsummer morning, and we arrived on a hilltop at dawn. The sky was clear; larks were pouring out their song and birds were flying around busily. When the shadow of the moon crept over the sun's face and the sky darkened, the birds returned to their nests, the larks dropped out of the sky, and an eerie silence fell. 'Darkness was on the face of the earth.' We waited and watched a sight we had never seen before, or would witness again – which ended in the coming of a second dawn, with the birds once more searching for food and the larks soaring in the sky. There could hardly have been a more convincing basis for the sun worship practised by so many races – which I met years later in the Inca remains of Macchu Picchu.

My father could not bear to be without somewhere to bathe. He had had the lake of Derwentwater and the de Navarros' pool in Broadway, so he proceeded to make a swimming-pool at Souldern Court. This gave endless pleasure to us and our visitors. He also planted a small orchard; and a severe drought set in, and he and the gardener were forced to water it day after day, in blazing heat. He then developed diabetes – thought to have been brought on by the anxiety and struggle of that time. In those days diabetes was incurable and, ultimately, fatal. The only hope of postponing the end was to adopt a diet so restricted in quantity as well as kind that it meant near-starvation. He put the letter-weighing machine in front of his place at table and weighed his food by ounces. Meals were an ordeal for us all. My father experienced – and, characteristically, exulted in – visions and hallucinations such as those described by fasting monks; but he became desperately close to a skeleton, and was weak and tired. The end seemed inevitable. However, at that moment came a miracle – the discovery of insulin. It gave him over twenty years of life, which he was well enough to enjoy.

By the mid-thirties life at Souldern had become impossibly expensive. It was necessary to economize, and I happened to be present when the subject made a painful appearance. The local flower show, held in the beautiful grounds of Aynho Park, was a great event at which we always won prizes. Our excellent gardener, Reeve, had it in his sights months ahead, and counted on achieving the longest string beans and the largest marrow. Of course every entry had a price-tag, and a few weeks before one show my father said that he thought we should make no entries. We couldn't afford it. My mother said that local activities should be the last things to go and that it would be a great blow to Reeve. My father insisted that we shouldn't spend the money. My mother said, 'It's my money. . . .' There was a silence, in which they each drew back from the brink of a precipice on which I got the impression they had never stood before nor would again. It was our last flower show. Souldern Court was put up for sale and my parents bought Epwell Mill, a few miles the other side of Banbury.

It was a small square millhouse, with the roofless stone walls of what had been a barn stretching away from it. My father engaged an architect who worked for the Historic Buildings Society to make from this a two-storey annexe. The first-floor library had to house the oak bookcases made for the Souldern library by the distinguished furniture designer Ernest Gimson. Its back window looked out over the millpond which, ten years earlier, my father would have made into a swimming-pool; but he no longer had the strength for ambitious projects.

Frequent visitors lamented the loss of Souldern, but several found Epwell even more to their liking. Souldern Court was in the middle of the village, while the millhouse was half a mile away from Epwell and there was not another building to be seen from its windows. The poet Robin Flower wrote of

> ... the intimacy of Epwell; the sense of being not only in the country, but *in* the country, with no tangible borders between the house and those enchanting hills and fields. I for one grow less responsive to the sensational landscape and more drawn to what the 18th century believed in – the peace that the world can give; and that is what we found at Epwell. I was very tired, and the absolute peace refreshed me beyond belief. The badger and the fox were unexpected; the little extra beyond the bargain, that makes perfection.

I have said nothing about my brother Michael since he was born in 1910. He was a charming little boy, whom Monica and I regarded rather as a toy. Although the gap between us sisters was almost as great, we had always done everything together. He was a young child when we went to boarding-school and it took several years before we realized that something was wrong. My father had always expected high standards of education and culture in those who surrounded him, and it had never occurred to him that any child of his would not attain those standards. But when the time came for Michael to go to boarding-school – the only possibility for those living in the country – one school after another asked for him to be removed because they could not teach him. I never really understood the problem. Michael was by no means stupid. He could be original and entertaining. He was even-tempered and kind. But he seemed to have no ability to use either hand or brain in any constructive way. I believe he was simply born into the wrong family: from childhood coming up against expectations he could not meet – while my father was incapable of modifying those expectations. The tragic result was that a black cloud hung over them. He lived with our parents because he could not live alone. My father withdrew into himself, except for occasional outbursts.

My mother was alone between them. What did they talk about over meals? There was no common ground; and people with close relationships cannot make small talk as they can with strangers. Monica and I were so concerned that we seriously discussed suggesting to our parents that they should separate: with our mother and Michael living together and our father living with her (my husband's parents were already living with us). But we never did so. They would not have agreed, and later experience showed that such an arrangement would not have worked anyway. The only consolation after our father's death was the belief that our mother and Michael would live happily together; so it was distressing to learn that he disliked feeling her presence anywhere in the house – which led her, in her mid-seventies, to spend hours in the garden, in all weathers.

In two years' time this situation, too, was resolved by our mother's death. I have often noticed that those who have had happy marriages, or close relations with parents, survive bereavement best, for they can look back without the remorse that besets those whose relationships have been less successful. My mother was the kindest and most unselfish of women; but she had never opened out to me – or I think, to anyone – so I never got near her and never helped her. And how much she had needed it was revealed when, after her death, I found in her jacket pockets scraps of paper on which she had scribbled, over and over again, 'Lord Jesus help me!' I can think of my father with a happy gratitude, because he gave me so much that has been the foundation of my life, and because he knew my love for him; but the knowledge that I failed my mother haunts me.

Michael settled in a nearby village. He never came to London to see us. He was on excellent terms with his neighbours and quite confident when he was in the area around him, but he didn't feel safe outside it. He died in his sleep of cerebral haemorrhage in 1955, aged forty-five.

3

The question of how I should earn my living was a difficult one, as my degree subjects did not lead to any profession. My principal interest was writing – other people's writing and, at the back of my mind, my own. My father's book, *Friends in Solitude*, was published by Jonathan Cape. I had an interview with the publishers; heard that there was no place for me; and was advised to get experience by working in a bookshop.

The first thing was to get settled in London, and I had friends who needed a fourth to take on some unfurnished rooms off the King's Road, Chelsea. My parents were abroad. I loaded furniture and luggage into their car and headed for London. I had hardly ever been there before and had never driven in a city. When I arrived at Marble Arch, I went round it twice before managing to exit down Park Lane and go on to Bramerton Street, where we each had a room and shared a tiny kitchen, with a bath behind a curtain beyond. When our social life was in full swing, those who were entertaining at home moved one another's pans off the gas rings, while those going out pushed through to wash. For some weeks I was the only one unemployed, so I had to cope with our very unpleasant landlord. After one particularly acrimonious encounter in the hall below, I went upstairs rather shaken. Our daily – a real Cockney, on the lines of George Belcher's *Punch* drawings – had been leaning over the banisters, drinking it in. She said, 'The 'orrible man. I 'eard 'im. I wish 'e was my 'usband!' I got a further glimpse into her home life when she complained of her husband stepping out of line:

'It's always me wot 'its the children.'

After Jonathan Cape had advised me to get a job in bookselling I applied to the most famous London bookshop of the day, J. & E. Bumpus, and got a job in the bound-book department, at 25 shillings a week. This was the department to which the wealthy and/or aristocratic brought their cloth-bound purchases for binding in half or full morocco, calf or pigskin, with or without some heraldic emblem. I was not an entirely welcome curiosity to the all-male staff. Of course they knew their regular customers well; new ones could be traced in *Debrett* or *Who's Who*; and they tried to teach me the rudiments of society. Dusting books at the end of the room I heard a hissing cry, 'Miss! Miss! Did you see the lady that passed through the department? No? What a pity! She was a typical knight's wife.'

Queen Mary came to Bumpus for small Christmas presents – and she shopped early, in the approved manner. One day in the first week of November, after opening Parliament in full regalia, she appeared at 2 p.m., dressed in purple from head to foot, topped by a toque made of pansies. She was accompanied by her private detective – a small, shy man, who confided to the staff that he had to do the near-impossible, not let the Queen out of his sight, yet keep out of her sight, as she disliked his presence. She came up to our department to examine our selection of booklets in pink or mauve limp suede, which contained small anthologies of poems. The series was called 'In a Nook', and among the titles were *In a Nook with a Lover* and *In a Nook with God*. Queen Mary ordered a dozen: no prizes for guessing which title she chose.

Quite early in my time at Bumpus I went to a concert in the Queen's Hall. As I sat alone in the gallery during the interval a young man came up to say hello. It was Jock Stewart, of the Bumpus staff. From then on we went to concerts together, and soon spent most of our free time in each other's company. His father was a professional musician who had played double-bass in the leading London orchestras but had to seek regular employment in Eastbourne. Jock had left school at seventeen, to earn a living. He was extremely intelligent, and embittered by the knowledge that he could have done at least as well as my college friends. Though very young, he was regarded as the best of

Bumpus's salesmen. He despised the job, yet lacked the self-confidence to go after anything else.

I still had my eye on publishing, and applied for a job in the advertising section of a small book publisher. I told them that I had no experience of advertising, but I got the job. After a few months they sacked me, saying that they needed an experienced man. That was the low point of my life and one I have never forgotten. The experience of unemployment can be even more painful than that of a marriage break-up or bereavement, because one has lost the foundation of one's life. It was 1931, a period of deep recession. I applied endlessly for jobs but got few replies. This went on for more than six months. One day I answered an advertisement for a sub-editor with a well-known fashion magazine, and was asked to an interview. The magazine was *Vogue*. My friends flocked round, offering an assortment of garments which we put together in the hope that I might make a good impression. I was interviewed by the managing editor, Miss Powell, whose manner and appearance were reassuringly human. I can't imagine why she took me on; but she did – and so began my thirty years with *Vogue*'s publishers, Condé Nast.

I started at £3 a week, my highest salary to date. The editorial department consisted of Miss Powell, me and a secretary. Between us we brought out the magazine every fortnight. It was wonderful good luck to be taught my new profession by Miss Powell. She had worked on the *Daily Telegraph* and was an accomplished professional, with a strong but calm personality, quiet humour and endless patience with me and the various, often temperamental, characters who blew in on us from other departments. I learnt how to write captions that exactly fitted the space which the art department had allotted on the layout. (If Miss Powell felt that more was needed she would do battle with the art editor.) In correcting proofs, one measured the type; but the typesetters at the printers would call up to protest at corrections made – as when I had marked the word 'knickers' to be split after the 'k' instead of before it, and got a call; 'Those knickers of yours, Miss Wivers. They won't split where you want them to.'

Miss Powell was scrupulous in not altering a contributor's copy without explanation, so one day she told me to call up the man who wrote our society piece. He was secretary of the Queen Charlotte Hospital, which had established the ritual that débutantes should begin their season there, by curtsying to a huge iced birthday cake before they danced the night away. Their chaperones were described by our contributor as sitting around the ballroom, 'la buste offrande'. She had consulted a dictionary and found that the word *buste* was masculine. 'Just ring him up, and tell him.' I did, nervously. 'What nonsense!' he shouted down the telephone. 'What could be more feminine!'

If I still had to find my feet in the office, I was an unsophisticated nitwit outside it. Frantic for someone to sign *Vogue*'s name as attending some cocktail party (the allotted staff member having been taken ill), I was dispatched to the Ritz, where I got wedged in a corner with a silent man. I tried to break the ice by stammering, 'I'm afraid I didn't catch your name.' The answer came back like a pistol-shot: 'The name is Coward.'

Just two years after my arrival Miss Powell had a cancer operation and, though it was successful, she took early retirement. I then became managing editor which, with us, was at the heart of the magazine's production. After the editorial conference, the editor and managing editor would assign a photographer or artist and a staff member to handle each feature. Schedules were issued, with dates for every stage of the proceedings. I felt like a juggler who keeps three balls in the air: one issue was being planned; material for its predecessor was coming in, and the third was on the verge of going to press.

In those days 'fashion' was an autocratic power. Twice a year the Paris collections, interpreted and publicized by the press, laid down 'The Look'. Fashion-conscious women would come to London in spring and autumn to buy their clothes and, before they bought, they would ask *Vogue* the position of the waist, the length of the skirt, the favourite fabrics and colours; and we could give confident rulings. This was a powerful incentive for buying the magazine, yet, now that women dress as they please, fashion magazines still command huge circulations. Of course publishing success comes from giving the public what it wants, and the present-day appetite is not for authority but for drama and excitement, with a dash of the outrageous.

A social editor was an important member of staff in the thirties, and that post was held by an American, Johnnie MacMullin. Through his close acquaintance with Mrs Simpson we had a front seat for the drama of her relationship with the King. One day he told us that he had sent her a cake for her birthday and asked if she had liked it. She replied that she had got only a pile of crumbs. The bodyguard, provided for fear of an attack, was so suspicious that he had sliced it to ribbons. When it came to their final elopement to France, we were able to publish a special coverage of the marriage and, later, of their Paris home. I found it both pathetic and distasteful that symbols of the Duke of Windsor's royal past figured throughout the furnishings. The three feathers of the Prince of Wales surmounted their bed and even the waste-paper baskets simulated the drums of the Brigade of Guards.

Johnnie was in demand for escorting ladies on expeditions, a demand that reached its apogee when he took two formidable ladies on visits to Indian rajas. They were high priestesses of the interior decoration cult. Syrie Maugham, ex-wife of Somerset Maugham, established the prevailing white of the time; while the American Elsie Mendl announced her taste when, on first seeing the Parthenon, she exclaimed, 'Beige! My colour!' In India, they travelled by train, changing their clothes aboard, to be correctly dressed for their arrival. On one occasion Ascot-type clothes with flowered hats were chosen. They were met by their raja host and his retinue, including a line of elephants. While the lengthy greetings went on, a bored elephant spotted a snack and, quietly stretching his trunk, lifted a hat from its wearer's head and munched it.

'Charisma' was not a word in use in those days, but the mysterious yet unmistakable quality it describes could be met from time to time, and I met it powerfully one evening at Cecil Beaton's house in Kensington. He had invited about a dozen people to meet Greta Garbo. We were standing around, talking and drinking, when she arrived. She sat in an armchair, conversation ceased and we all simply gravitated towards her – some pulling up chairs, others sitting on the floor. She was wearing a plain, high-necked black sweater and black skirt, no jewellery, no make-up. She answered the odd question with a few words, saying nothing memorable or even interesting, yet we were all riveted. There seemed to be nobody else in the room.

Cecil's own gifts were uniquely varied and numerous: he was a photographer, artist, writer, stage and costume designer, as well as interior decorator. He set the stamp of his personality on everything he did: his photographs of Queen Elizabeth as the consort of King George VI, and his designs for Audrey Hepburn in *My Fair Lady*, are expressive of an era. It was appropriate that Roy Strong, when director of the National Portrait Gallery, chose Beaton's work for its first photographic exhibition, recognizing the fact that the personalities of our age are more likely to be remembered by photographs than by portraits.

Before the war the relationship between British *Vogue* and the New York office resembled that of parent and adolescent child. The Americans didn't really believe that we could be trusted to do anything important without supervision. Our proprietor, Condé Nast, and the American *Vogue* editor, Edna Chase, visited London and Paris each year and put the staff through their paces. Our board – two men and one woman – would go to Waterloo to meet the boat-train. Alison Settle, the editor, told me that while taking Mr Nast's secretary to her modest hotel (he stayed at the Ritz) she asked her whether she had enjoyed the voyage. 'Well, Mr Nast was dictating all the way over. I didn't have time to look out of the porthole.' Alison tried again: 'The country coming up in the train must have been looking pretty?' 'I'm afraid I didn't see it. Mr Nast was dictating all the way up.' My position in the hierarchy involved no more than tea with Mr Nast; but the directors took him to the theatre, then to a night-club, and around midnight he would talk about the company's balance sheet. It took the enforced separation of the war years to persuade them that we had grown up. They were impressed that we had survived and even succeeded, and a new element of respect crept into the relationship.

In my early days at *Vogue*, when our offices and photographic studio were in the same building, an occasional story from a sitting filtered through to us. The photographer was king. What-ever he wanted, he had to have – and this entailed certain models and certain editors. A colleague on the fashion staff put in a chit for expenses incurred in resuscitating a model who had been greeted by a Paris photographer with the cry 'Who's that cow? Take her away!' This pre-eminence persists, because it is the photographs which make a fashion magazine exciting, while a catalogue is simply informative. Photographers have brainwaves, and these have to be examined seriously, though not always acted on. One of Norman Parkinson's brainwaves was to hire two helicopters, one for a model and one for himself, who were to lean out of their respective aircraft while hovering over the Houses of Parliament. A refusal on grounds of prohibitive cost would have been thought unimaginative and mean. Fortunately I found that commercial aircraft were not permitted in that particular airspace.

It was also the day of the fashion artist: Bérard, the most famous, but Carl Erickson ('Eric'), Willaumez and René Bouché the finest in that field. To my mind, Eric in particular – whose drawings often showed figures in a drawing-room or theatre foyer – left records of the period that far surpass photographs. And he could conjure up a scene in real life, too. He was in London at the time of the Queen's coronation and I took him out to lunch. He had heard a military band marching through the streets and reproduced the effect for my benefit. He began with the band in the distance, coming nearer and louder until it was just beside him, and then fading away. The entire restaurant was riveted; every knife and fork was laid down, conversation ceased – but Eric was too absorbed to notice the sensation he was making.

I was privileged to be an onlooker at a photographic session of Irving Penn, in my opinion the greatest photographer of our time. He asked me to sit at the back of the studio and to keep quiet. For the first ten minutes or so he tried changes in the girl's pose; then he held one, and began a monologue of which I could not hear a word, but which reminded me, in its privacy and intensity, of the questioning priest in a marriage service. All the time he was taking pictures, and sheets of contact prints would be on my desk next day, almost identical but subtly different. One or two would catch one's eye – something arresting in the girl's expression. The business people at Condé Nast begged me to ask Penn to use less film, but I had enough respect for the creative process to know that a few rolls of film were a small price to pay for the masterpieces that were Penn photographs.

Homosexuality was a criminal offence, yet the minor arts of fashion design, interior decoration and photography were dominated by homosexuals. They were much treasured in society as delightful and valuable companions – attentive and amusing, and expert in subjects of great concern to women. In general, we did not appreciate the perpetual strain they endured, that of possible blackmail and ruin. But this struck me hard after a visit to Venice, where I had come across the owner of a London art gallery I often visited. He invited me to dine in his apartment and sent me back to my *pensione* in his private gondola, rowed by two handsome young men in dashing uniforms. They were his lovers; they began to blackmail him; and a few weeks later he committed suicide.

I think it was the sense of insecurity, and an understandable resentment against society, that sometimes brought in an element of treachery – of biting the hand that fed them. The most sensational example of this was shown in American *Vogue*. Cecil Beaton spent a period in New York each year. Edna Chase told me that, a week after his arrival, he could tell her more about its up-an-coming life than her resident staff. During one visit he was commissioned to sketch in several New York restaurants. No one bothered to read the words he had scribbled beside each drawing, but they were read when the issue came out, and the telephone never stopped ringing. One restaurant was described as 'the haunt of all the —— Yids in town'; a large proportion of American *Vogue*'s advertisers were Jewish firms, and they were cancelling their advertisements.

Of course the various *Vogue* offices provided each other with material. When it came to the coronation of George VI, American *Vogue* wanted to introduce their readers to an unfamiliar royal couple. We met such demands as we could, but drew the line at one that asked for photographs of 'models chatting to the sentries outside Buckingham Palace', and another 'of the crown jewels on the Queen's dressing table'. Our New York colleagues thought us feeble and uncooperative, so a tit-for-tat incident was rather amusing. On the eve of a presidential election American *Vogue* provided themselves and us with a feature on the favoured candidate, Thomas Dewey; so Truman's election brought editorial as well as political dismay. The Trumans were relatively unknown to us, so we asked for Mrs Truman to be interviewed and photographed. Edna Chase sent us the brief cable reply, 'No interviews – Bess Truman', covering her chagrin at not supplying the material by calling it a welcome change from the self-publicizing Roosevelts, who were detested by our New York management.

Eleanor Roosevelt, who was a considerable personality in her own right, visited London during the war and was the guest of honour at the opening of the Women's Press Club in the City, which I had helped to found. Naturally, the absence of men meant more women journalists in Fleet Street; their work often went on into the night and there was nowhere for them to eat or rest – the Press Club being restricted to men only. Those of us who had a pull with firms making household goods used it to get the club furnished and its kitchen equipped, and we drew upon the expertise of members to get it up and running. I remember a journalist from *Good Housekeeping*, who overlooked the cooking arrangements, warning us that a splash of fat the size of a shilling could support a fast-breeding family of cockroaches.

To return to my private life. The Bramerton Street ménage had broken up, as do all such groups, through marriage or job change, and a pair of us moved to Paddington Green. The sole buildings there were an eighteenth-century church, a three-house terrace of the same period – where we had a flat – and a children's hospital. (Only church and hospital survived the bombing.) My flat-mate, who designed theatrical costumes, knew Bernard Miles, creator of the Mermaid Theatre. He and his wife had a house in St John's Wood Road with a large barn in the garden which, characteristically, he had turned into a theatre. I went to some of the productions he staged there, of which the most remarkable was the Purcell opera, *Dido and Aeneas* – beautiful enough in itself but made even more memorable by the personality of the soprano. Bernard had persuaded his friend Kirsten

Flagstad to play Dido; her fee, a pint of Guinness. It was a miracle that she, who filled the expanse of Covent Garden in her roles as Isolde or Brünnhilde, could modify that marvellous voice to personify Dido, in a barn.

Our friends had assumed that Jock and I would marry, and one day we did. From my parents' point of view it must have been an unsatisfactory affair, to a man they had never taken to, and not in church but at a registry office. The maisonette above my flat in Paddington Green had fallen empty and we moved in there – to be joined by Jock's parents. Eastbourne, like other south coast towns, was saving money by disbanding its orchestra. I was grateful for my mother-in-law's help in housekeeping. In those days shops had not opened when one left for work in the morning, and they were shut by the time one returned.

The wages and prices of the past are far removed from those of the present, but in fact they bear a fairly constant relation to one another. I could not have lived on my first weekly wage of 25 shillings but, supplemented by my £100-a-year private income (from an uncle's gift of shares in the family company), I could pay my share of a 3/-6 dinner, with a glass of wine, in Soho, and then a gallery seat at the theatre. One could dance all night for 2/-6 – either at Olympia, where the huge area needed two bands, always out of rhythm with one another, or at Covent Garden, where the stalls were boarded over with a dance floor for much of the year.

In 1938 the lease of our Paddington Green maisonette came to an end and we moved to a house on the Regent's Canal – not at all the prestigious Little Venice of today. It was in a curved terrace facing the Paddington Basin and belonged to the council. The interior was dingy and dilapidated; every room had a different tenant, each cooking on a gas ring and sharing a bathroom; but the view was stunning. A very old member of the Bumpus staff heard where we were going and remarked, 'Mr Browning used to live there. I knew him when I was a boy.' 'Robert Browning? Really? How interesting!' 'Yes, I knew him very well. I used to take him maggots for his owl.'

Before long, war broke out. In the first weeks we slept on the ground floor, but soon gave that up. Actually, our only bomb damage was shattered window glass. The waterway traffic was fascinating. Tons of rubbish were loaded on to barges in the Paddington Basin and a procession of them would move off up the canal. In rainy weather the crews opened umbrellas, the scene resembling a black-and-white Japanese print. It is difficult for anyone who has not experienced some powerful event – bereavement, bankruptcy, unemployment – to understand what it feels like. The same could be said of war. I have no conception what it is like to fight with a tangible enemy, but I do know what it is to live in a country at war and in a city under bombardment. No one close to me was in any more danger than I was, so perhaps it will not sound too outrageous if I say that my personal experience was exhilarating, because life had a new value. I woke up every morning with the delighted consciousness of being alive and with a strong sense of purpose. Everyday affairs – usually carried out unthinkingly – became a challenging obstacle race that one rejoiced at winning.

After the fatal meeting of Hitler and Chamberlain at Munich in 1938, when I – and hundreds of thousands of others – felt no relief but only a conviction that war would come, I joined the Auxiliary Fire Service as a driver. I saw myself driving a fire-engine and, in the office lunch-hour, took lessons in driving heavy vehicles round the back streets of Chelsea. I got my HV (heavy vehicle) driving licence but never drove anything larger than an ancient taxi, in which I ferried officers between fire stations. It dated from before the days of self-starters, so I had to crank it by hand; and taxi-drivers were not mollycoddled by doors and windows; my seat was wide open to every wind that blew.

The most eerie experience for me, and no doubt for my passengers, was in the early days of the war, when the great fear was of a gas attack, and I was instructed to transport a group of officers – all of us wearing gas masks. There were no street lights. Traffic lights were blacked out, with only a cross-slit showing a glimmer – which was all that the car lights gave. Advice had not reached us that a gas mask would mist up unless the lenses were rubbed with soap, so before long I was the blind driving the blind. There was no ditch to fall into, but there was a tense moment when, in making a right-hand turn, I found myself across the bonnet of a bus, which also had minimal lighting but was fortunately going slowly. As I was at the office all day – and with a skeleton staff at that – my fire-service driving was at night. When my stint was over in the early hours I would walk back, often through air raids, to our house on the Regent's Canal. It was a beautiful scene, with tracer bullets from anti-aircraft guns going up among the huge silver barrage balloons that hung above the city.

A night to remember was one on which the sky in the east was such a brilliant red that the leaves on the plane trees lining the canal stood out black against it. In the morning we learnt that a great fire had raged after the bombing of the City, which had left St Paul's standing among acres of devastation. Much later I was told a story by a friend of a friend who had been nearer to the action that night. He was on Winston Churchill's staff and, typically, his boss meant to have a sight of the drama. A group of them climbed out on to the flat roof of their building, which gave an upper-circle vantage-point for the spectacle. In the darkness Churchill bumped into some sort of protuberance and sat on it. After a while a nervous little clerk appeared from below, found his way to the Prime Minister and said apologetically, 'Excuse me, sir, but my room is full of smoke.' Churchill launched into an impassioned speech: 'The great city is burning. Even as we watch, centuries of our heritage go up in flames – and you tell me that your room is full of smoke!' 'Yes, sir, I know. But you see, you are sitting on my chimney.'

Another Churchill story – this time, some years after the war – concerns a fellow-member of a committee, who described how he had been roaming round the upper floors of the House of Commons, looking for the room of his MP. As he hesitated in the corridor he heard a door shut, and there was a strong smell of cigar-smoke. It flashed across his mind that it could be Churchill, and it was. He flattened himself against the wall, expecting the Prime Minister to pass; but he stopped, stared, and said, 'I know you.' My acquaintance told me that he could only stammer idiotically, 'I don't think you do, sir, but I know you.' Churchill was not to be put off. He went on staring, and said, 'I met you

when I visited the army in Egypt, before the Battle of Alamein.'
And it was true that he had been one of the many officers
introduced to Churchill.

We were on the south coast for the weekend, after the fall of
France, when a German invasion was expected at any moment.
Walking on the Downs we came across a solitary lad in uniform,
standing beside a gun. He was glad to have someone to talk to
and soon dropped his voice to a whisper, confiding, 'I wouldn't
like to be 'itler. We've got a machine-gun every mile along this
coast.' After this reassuring news we left him to his confident
vigil. I think British strength in times of crisis comes from being
short on imagination. The Home Guard (Dad's Army) was never
issued with enough guns to go round, or with ammunition for
practice shooting, because sufficient supplies didn't exist, but
they cheerfully turned up for 'training' – also probably feeling
sorry for Hitler having to face them. Almost every quality has its
plus and minus sides; and while lack of imagination is usually a
failing, it can, in some circumstances, be a salvation.

In those days the London Zoo was open on Sunday mornings
to Fellows of the Royal Zoological Society. I knew Barbara
Castle and her husband very slightly and they invited me to join
them there one Sunday. In the brown bears' enclosure there was
a solitary man whom we watched in fascinated silence. In one
hand he held a long stick with a wooden spoon lashed to the end.
In the other was a large tin of Golden Syrup, from which he
offered a spoonful to a bear standing on its hind legs and rolling
its tongue round every inch of that spoon. The other bears were
standing patiently, not jostling or shoving; and when one had
had its spoonful it moved off and another took its place. The
brilliant 'points' system made shopping for food far better in the
Second World War than in the First, because it allowed people of
different tastes and needs to spend their coupons in their preferred way. The bears' friend must have been a bachelor, able to
indulge in a reckless expenditure of points on Golden Syrup.
Barbara Castle and I, as housewives, could appreciate the extent
of his devotion.

Marghanita Laski was an outstanding personality who often
wrote for us, and with whom I became friendly. I am not prone

to believe in fortune-telling, but I shared an unusual experience with her in the booth of a fortune-teller on a Hampstead Heath bank holiday. She and her husband and two young children had been strolling round the fair with Jock and me when she spotted a fortune-telling sign pointing down a distant avenue of caravans. She took me off with her, while the others went in the opposite direction. The gypsies were sitting inside their caravans, and ours set out to tell me the usual rambling, unconvincing tale. Marghanita was getting much the same treatment when she broke in with, 'Shall I have any children?' The gypsy's singsong delivery suddenly changed to that of everyday conversation when she gave her quick reply: 'Well, you have two already. You don't want any more, do you?'

The first weeks of the war had brought no gas attacks or bombing raids or troop movements. Life went on normally – so normally that, early in 1940, my American editor told me that she intended to go back to the States for several months, to renew contacts with the New York office and handle family affairs. But first she would visit the Paris collections and then go on to Italy – where she only just caught the last boat from Genoa, because the 'phoney war' had become a reality. Betty Penrose was a brave woman, devoted to her job and happy in England. She had every intention of returning; but the bombing began, the State Department refused to release her passport, and the company found her the editorship of one of their American magazines. So my managing director said that he supposed I had better go on editing *Vogue*, as I had been doing for the past six months. He put me on the board to keep him company, as the American advertising director had also gone home, and with no intention of returning. Even after the war, when the board membership grew to six, I was still the only woman director and the only representative of the editorial side of the company. I thought, and said, that that was wrong. The editors of other magazines should have been there, and heads of editorial departments should have been brought in when subjects affecting them were discussed. As it was, I had to represent them as best I could, and pass on sometimes unwelcome decisions which they had had no opportunity to question. I hope that, since those far-off days, more 'open government' has come to British boardrooms.

My position at *Vogue* was yet another example of my extraordinary luck in being in the right place at the right time. Only two years after my arrival at Condé Nast I had stepped into the shoes of my sick managing editor. Now I was stepping into the shoes of my war-casualty editor, whom in the normal course of events I could not have succeeded, as she was so near my own age. What would, in ordinary circumstances, have been an upheaval for me and for the staff, was simply business as usual.

Women's magazines had a special place in government thinking during the war because, with men in the forces, women carried the whole responsibility of family life; and the way to catch women's attention was through the pages of magazines which, in total, were read by almost every woman in the country. So a group of editors were frequently invited to briefings by ministries that wanted to get across information and advice on health, food, clothing and so on. And they sought advice from us too – telling us what they wanted to achieve and asking how best to achieve it. We were even appealed to on fashion grounds. The current vogue was for shoulder-length hair. Girls working in factories refused to wear the ugly caps provided, with the result that their hair caught in machines and there were horrible scalping accidents. Could we persuade girls that short hair was chic? We thought we could, and featured the trim heads of the actresses Deborah Kerr and Coral Browne to prove it. But what about also designing more attractive caps?

Editors of magazines specially concerned with fashion were much in demand at the Board of Trade, where they were setting up the utility clothing scheme, designed to save both fabric and labour. Maximum yardage was laid down, and the maximum number of buttons and buttonholes, pockets and pleats. Men's trousers could no longer have turn-ups; but some men, even more fashion conscious than women, got their tailors to make their trousers too long, and then took them to a 'little man' to turn them up. The utility scheme brought anguished cries from some designers, but it did a great service to British fashion, which had been far too elaborate and fussy for its health, and was now forced to look for the attractions of simplicity.

There are social problems in every country, at every time, but it seems that one can count on efforts to solve them only in times of crisis. Because women were badly needed outside the home, crèches and nursery schools sprang up everywhere (they were rapidly closed when the war ended). Because it was essential to keep everyone healthy, great trouble was taken to ensure that children were vaccinated, and inoculated against infectious diseases. School meals were, I think, universal. Milk, in third-of-a-pint bottles, was distributed to schools. I even had a hand in this. When I was staying with cousins in North Wales, whose farm supplied such milk, their French governess-cum-dairymaid had to nurse a child ill with typhoid, so I was co-opted, picking up procedures shouted from the required distance in a strong French accent.

Our greatest publishing excitement of the war came about through Lee Miller – one of the gifted Americans who had been drawn by the magnetic power of Paris between the wars. Working in the studio of Man Ray, she had herself become a fine photographer; and she came to London in 1939 to work for us. When American forces arrived in Britain, Lee became attached to the US War Department. Only about a month after D-Day she crossed the Channel with them, and a stream of photographs began to arrive at the Ministry of Information. When a fresh batch passed through the censorship, I would go to collect them. With one batch, taken during the siege of St Malo, we were struck by the strange shape of the shell-bursts in the sky. Then the telephone rang and an agitated voice told me to bring back the photographs immediately. They took away every one which showed those shell-bursts; the explosive used was on the secret list.

Lee shared in the triumphant liberation of Paris, where she had joyous reunions with former friends, and then she went on to the crossing of the Rhine and the horror of Buchenwald. That was our first sight of the concentration camps, and now that they have passed into history it is difficult to convey the shock of that unimaginable nightmare. This was brought to us not only by her photographs but by the vivid writing that accompanied them. She sent us articles of several thousand words, and I had the problem of cutting them, because paper was strictly rationed. All users of paper were allowed a percentage of their 1938 consumption, and this percentage dropped to 18 per cent. One dissenting, 'privileged' voice spoke out in the House of Commons, and was directed at us. Eleanor Rathbone, a distinguished Labour MP, protested that the *Channel Islands Gazette* had been refused a paper quota, whereas one had been given to that 'pernicious magazine, *Vogue*'. We had to grin and bear the unfair adjective Miss Rathbone had pinned on us.

It was in this acutely rationed situation that I wrestled with Lee's absorbing articles. It is always painful to cut good writing, but particularly in this case, for I felt that Lee's features gave *Vogue* a validity in wartime it would not otherwise have had. It was all very well encouraging ourselves with the conventional patter about keeping up morale, providing entertainment and so on, but magazines – unlike books – are essentially about the here and now. And this was wartime, Lee's photographs and reports taking the magazine right into the heart of the conflict. I much regretted that, in a splendid photographic exhibition called *Seventy-five Years of Vogue* at the Royal College of Art in 1991, there was not a single photograph from the war period of any subject except fashion and personalities.

When the war ended, Lee travelled on into Eastern Europe where, in a remote Romanian village, she went down with severe back trouble. She knew that Romanian gypsies trained bears as masseuses, and she lay flat on her face on the floor for the treatment. She wrote: 'The bear knew her job. She walked up and down my back as gently as if on eggs, and the weight, 300 pounds of it, was transferred from foot to foot with very little change of pressure. She sat her great furry warm bottom down on the nape of my neck, and with gentle strides went from my neck to my knees and back again. It was crushing and exhilarating.'

While Lee Miller was covering the war and its aftermath in Europe, Cecil Beaton was an official war photographer in North Africa and, later, in India and China. He possessed the triple gifts of drawing, writing and photography, and made it possible for us to report on large areas of the world while held in our beleaguered island.

I am very well aware that I would not have been an appropriate editor of *Vogue* at any other period of its history. I had come up through copy-writing and administration, with no fashion training. My managing director, Harry Yoxall, told me at the start that there were basically two kinds of editors: one who went out and about, keeping an ear to the ground and coming back with good stories which the staff worked on; the other stayed at home, sifted material brought in by staff, and shaped it for publication. I was never in any doubt that I fell into that second category, which meant of course that I needed a very high quality in my principal colleagues in our various departments. I went to fashion shows in London and to the Paris collections, but I set special store by the quality of the fashion staff. I needed to rely on their taste and judgement, and that ability to spot future trends which is the key to success in matters concerning design. Pat Cunningham, fashion editor for most of the period, and her colleagues Sheila Wetton and Unity Barnes, possessed those qualities. Sheila had been a model at Molyneux, and came to us when he wound up his London business to concentrate on Paris. She had a fund of stories of life behind the scenes in a couture house. One *nouvelle-riche* customer used to arrive clutching a clean corset wrapped in newspaper, explaining, 'My fitter likes me fresh.' And when the sewing-rooms produced a dress for an extremely large customer, Sheila and another mannequin got inside it together, taking one sleeve each, and waltzed wildly round the showroom.

Producing a magazine is a perpetual creative process, and every member of the editorial staff contributes to the final mosaic. All who go out-and-about have to possess a multiplicity of talents: taste, expertise, determination, the ability to win co-operation from all those with whom they work – the companies whose products they have chosen to feature, the personalities, photographers, artists, models. Those whose work is office-bound then play their part. The art department can work wonders with imaginative layouts. A straightforward piece of fashion copy grabs attention by an arresting headline.

It was the job of my colleagues in the various departments to draw upon the areas of their special interest. And it was my job to bring all their contributions together, making a magazine which would catch and hold the attention of readers, and so produce the circulation and attract the advertising which a publishing company needs for success. Before each editorial conference, the heads of departments would talk to me about the subjects they wanted to cover, and the space these would take. The fashion editor produced her menu. We always included pages for readers on tight budgets and for the older woman (I can't remember why she had been christened 'Mrs Exeter', but she was much respected). The beauty editor would promote new make-up or hair-styles. The feature editor would want her Spotlight article to be illustrated by photographs of personalities in the news, or with reproductions from art exhibitions. They all had to begin by selling their ideas to me; and, when we had agreed on them, we got down to the business of selling them to our readers.

In preparation for an editorial conference I would set up a board showing what was proposed. The entire editorial staff attended the conference, and would raise arguments as to whether the appropriate number of pages was being given to a feature, whether some excluded subject should be brought in, and so on. The next stage was between me and the managing editor: allotting work to staff members and to photographers and artists (all under contract to us). The managing editor then drew up individual schedules with dates for photographic sittings – allowing for retakes, if necessary, giving time for making layouts, writing copy, reading and correcting proofs. All this against a deadline which ensured that the printers would deliver copies for the publication date. We were quite proud that only three times during the war did we overrun that date.

All day, every day, colleagues would drop in to discuss changes and developments in their assignments. The magazine's character was to lead, always to be the first to spot a trend or to celebrate a new achievement, so plans needed to remain fluid. Sheets of contact prints of every sitting went the rounds. Copy came to me from everyone writing it; and I read, three times, every word that went into the magazine – first in typescript, then in proof, and finally before it went to press. The sheer volume of the work meant that I often left the office long after it had officially closed:

a habit noticed by an unlikely character, the newspaper seller at the arch into Regent Street from Golden Square, where *Vogue* had its post-war home. One night as I bought my paper, he said, 'I saw your light go out and reckoned you'd be along.' As my office was on the second floor of a building at the far end of the square, and our previous conversation had not gone beyond 'Good evening', I was taken aback. One imagines that one is anonymous in a city; but it was apparent that observers could tell a tale before the days of video cameras.

The quality of staff is the most important factor in any enterprise, and good staff need to feel appreciated and listened to, which some managers do not always realize. In my early days at *Vogue* I heard the editor end a discussion in which she stated her overruling decision with the words, 'What's the good of being an editor if you can't have your own way?' Even then I remember rejecting that job description; and when I became an editor I tried never to overrule any member of my staff on the ground of personal taste. Sheets of contact prints would make the rounds, showing the initialled choices of the photographer, the editor-in-charge, the art editor and, finally, of myself. I knew that all of them cared about what was chosen, and would have been no good at their job if they hadn't cared. When opposing votes had to be reconciled – and perhaps opposed altogether – I took trouble to give an objective reason: the impact on the reader, the clarity of the information, and so on. Of course an editor is responsible for everything that appears in a paper, and an editor's decision is final; but that decision can be reached in various ways, and I did not think an autocratic way was the best one.

It was a shock, then, to find that the earlier editor description was alive and well in Paris. The editor of French *Vogue*, Michel de Brunhoff, was the brother of Jean, creator of Babar. He was a tremendous character and a highly cultured man. One day, when he was out at a long French lunch, I went in to his office and saw a variety of cover layouts on the wall. One of the staff explained that Michel had asked five of them to vote for their choice. They all chose the same shot, but Michel voted for another, and announced, 'The editor's vote counts for six.' He ranked nations from a cultural viewpoint, with France at the top and Britain near the bottom. He had no wish for news of artistic developments we had made during the war years. The New York office had made an imaginative appointment in sending a gifted young woman, Rosamond Riley (who, later, with her French husband, founded and edited the art magazine *L'Oeil*), to report on such developments in France and England. I had introduced her to Graham Sutherland and Henry Moore, and she took photographs of their work to Paris. But Michel said, 'I don't associate England with art. I associate it with débutantes in long white dresses, sitting on green grass' – the Beaton syndrome no doubt.

I saw quite a lot of Graham Sutherland and his wife, visiting them at their country house and taking them to the first night of Benjamin Britten's *Rape of Lucretia*. After my divorce, when they were living in France, I didn't contact them because I felt that, as Roman Catholics, they would disapprove. But I liked them very much and must have written several years later, for I have Graham's reply: 'Thank you so much for your sweet letter. We had heard that you and Jock had parted, and also that you felt sensitive as to the possibility of coldness from us as a result. You really did not have to worry at all; for we count you among our warmest and sweetest friends. I had heard that you had remarried and were very happy – and we are both so happy for you.'

My luck as an editor was mainly because the 1940s and 1950s were exceptional years that happened to chime in with my personal interest in features. Fashion was naturally at a low ebb, and it did not fully recover until I was about to bow out. During the war, and until paper stocks were normal again, the magazine was available only to subscribers and, until one of them died (it was inconceivable that anyone would give it up), no new subscriber could be taken on. So it was a perfect period to include more features than would usually be wise, taking account of the magazine's circulation and profitability. Alexander Liberman, the highly influential art director of American *Vogue*, wrote a series of articles on modern painters, each faced by a full-page colour reproduction. Kingsley Amis wrote an article which we described as 'militating against the contemporary school of impertinent prudery that he calls Neo-Puritanism'. We celebrated the very different seasons of Gian-Carlo Menotti and John Christie, saying of Glyndebourne: 'Urged on by Christie, singers turn into democrats and Englishmen into opera afficionados: twin un-likelihoods from which proceeds the miracle that an opera company can flourish without a penny from the Arts Council.' I enjoyed a remarkable series of feature editors: Lesley Blanch, Siriol Hugh Jones, Penelope Gilliatt – all outstanding person-alities and writers who had the confidence of people in the theatre and cinema, music and art. They had appreciative col-leagues in the art editor and me, and the space to spread them-selves; so we all enjoyed it. I think it could be said that, during this unusual period in *Vogue's* history, it became The Intelligent Woman's Guide to much more than fashion.

I am responsible for the fact that we never published an article by Graham Greene. I asked him to write one for the opening spread of a Christmas issue, facing a colour page of a Carlo Crevelli *Madonna and Child*. Of course I had told him of the context in which his article would be used; but to my dismay it dwelt upon the agonies of the Crucifixion, and I had to tell him that I found it unsuitable. I think I ought to have known better than to expect a conventional Christmas approach from him.

I spent many wartime lunch-hours in the art galleries that cluster around Bond Street, and returned one day to give the art editor good news. We were desperate for fashion artists and I had seen, in his first exhibition, the work of an artist who could draw tweed. I still maintain that I had grounds for that convic-tion; but fortunately we took the notion no further, and his next show killed it dead. It was Francis Bacon.

I was not so foolish as to ask Bernard Shaw to write for us; but I did ask him to let us send a photographer to his house. In response I received one of his famous postcards. It read: 'My wife's years and my own exceed 170. Cameramen are most unwelcome and are in fact not admitted. *Vogue* is ten years too late.' He was a figure recognized to an extent that no writer would be today. I saw him when he was very old, drifting down Pall Mall. Everyone turned to look at him and even the passing taxis slowed down. I loved a story about an incident in his old age, when he was bathing off the coast of South Africa. He was floating in the sunshine when a boy swam near, and then veered away. 'What's up?' he asked. 'Chaps on the beach bet that I wouldn't dare duck you – but I'm not having any.' 'Hold on!' said Shaw. 'That's easy money. Just give me time to get my breath, and you can push my head under.' Not many of the world's greats would have been so practical and unpretentious.

Two future Royal Academicians made drawings for us. John Ward's gift for subjects that might be called 'Landscape with Figures' was right up our street, and gave us some charming portrayals of people in their homes or gardens. Ruskin Spear was, at that stage, a young artist ready to try his hand at anything. He found fashion sittings hilarious; but later settled for subject-matter where he felt more at home – such as scenes in streets and pubs.

Printing costs varied widely from one region to another, and naturally London was particularly expensive; so the magazine was printed by a family firm with whom we became very friendly. This was all very well in normal times when vans ran to and fro; but in wartime, with petrol rationing, the only transport was by train. We would get a telephone call saying that a packet of proofs had been put on a certain train, and one of us would go to Euston to collect it, and return there to send back new copy or corrected proofs. When the war ended we were given a conducted tour of what had been a top-secret area, where they printed the pamphlets which Allied planes scattered over France. They were produced by Free French journalists and were illustrated in colour: no restrictions for them, with paper or colour printing. They were very well done, and I hope that specimens remain in the wartime archives.

It is sometimes said that problems such as sexual harassment have always existed, and only surface now because of the greater openness of our time. I can only say that I had never met it before – and nor had a member of my fashion staff, when she came to complain about the behaviour of a certain ready-to-wear manufacturer who was an important advertiser. I asked him to come and see me, and he naturally thought I wanted to talk about his collection – but I broke in with the tale I had been told, said that such behaviour was unacceptable and, if it happened again, I would not allow members of my staff to visit his salon. There was a risk that he would storm out and cancel his advertising; but to my relief he muttered an apology and made for the door.

Wars shake the whole structure of a country and have a profound effect on social attitudes. Society with a capital 's' never regained its position when peace returned, so *Vogue* did not appoint a post-war social editor. Instead, we had a freelance relationship with one or two women who could use their influence in getting aristocratic beauties to pose for us, or in opening the doors of handsome houses for our interior decoration features. Among these was Loelia, Duchess of Westminster (there was more than one such duchess at that time); and it is to her that I owe a remarkable experience. Mr Paul Getty was a neighbour of hers in Kent; and, while staying with her for the weekend, she rang him up to ask whether she might bring her guests to see his wonderful collection displayed there. We enjoyed a very special private view. Paintings on the walls of a house have an impact greater than when hanging in a public gallery, but I should also dearly like to visit the Getty Museum in Malibu.

Soon after the war we heard that American *Vogue* had brought out a book on etiquette. A copy was sent to us, and we read it with mingled mirth and alarm: alarm that copies might reach England and we should never hear the end of it. Just one of its maxims remains with me, from a chapter on etiquette while in mourning: 'It is incorrect to wear a mourning band when you are in hunting pink.' But I ought to have taken more seriously a chapter that set out the correct lengths of time to be late for every conceivable social function; because when Victor (my second husband) and I were invited to a cocktail party in New York, and his fanatical punctuality brought us to the door at the appointed hour, we were told that our hostess was having a bath.

I was quite often invited to give talks to lunch clubs and design schools on aspects of *Vogue* life, but an unusual assignment from the BBC World Service was to give a series of broadcasts on wartime and post-war life in England – to the Far East. 'Do you mean India?' I asked. 'Oh no! Further east than that.' I went to Bush House to discuss the project with a Mr Mac——, and was directed to a floor where I found myself already in the Far East, as it was completely inhabited by Burmese. They gathered round and helpfully looked up the name in their records, but as these all began with 'U' (as in U Thant, secretary-general of the United Nations) we concluded that I had better go back to reception. I was also a member, with Peter Ustinov, of a quiz show panel at the English Speaking Union. Of course Ustinov stole the show, to the delight of all concerned. Shortly after the war there was great nervousness about the possible spread of disease through air travel, and everyone entering the United States had to show a recent vaccination certificate. Peter Ustinov described a police-man going through his plane, demanding to see each passenger's certificate. He himself hadn't got one, but talked his way out of it – which emboldened a girl beside him to say hopefully that she hadn't got one either. Upon which the policeman – a King Kong of a man – seized her by the arm, lifted her off the ground and carried her away, announcing, 'Sister, you and me's going to get vaccinated.'

I thought this was a perfect example of that unfair fact of life that some people can get away with murder and others with not the slightest fault; and it's just as well to know to which category you belong. *Vogue* was strict about time-keeping: that is to say, about arriving on time in the morning though not about leaving in the evening. One of my colleagues had such riveting tales of the occurrences which habitually made her late that everyone just laughed; but when I bumped into the managing director as I got out of the lift, and apologized for lateness on account of a bus strike, all I got was, 'Have you no alternative transport?'

4

In September 1945, three months after the war ended, I went to Paris to see our colleagues on French *Vogue*. It was extraordinary to be crossing the Channel again, after five years of isolation. On board the ferry we were issued with life-jackets and instructions on procedure if the boat were to strike one of the mines that had been strewn around, in fear of invasion. The train from the coast to Paris crawled and stopped frequently, on account of the damage that our air raids had spent several years inflicting on the French rail system. I was met in Paris by the editor of French *Vogue*, Michel de Brunhoff, in a small car he shared with a colleague. It was no problem to take on board a large trunk I had brought, filled with gifts for the French staff, because the passenger seat beside the driver had long been removed to make room for a sack of farm produce. Michel told me that, at the beginning of the war, he and his wife had foreseen bad times ahead and had bought dozens of pairs of socks as barter currency. Every few weeks they would drive into the country in search of vegetables, perhaps some eggs or a bird, for which they traded socks.

The magazine itself had had to close, but they had brought out one or two fashion albums. And fashion in Paris, as I saw it then, was a remarkable vindication of the belief expressed so convincingly by James Laver, a member of staff of the V & A and writer on fashion – that not only our needs but our whole outlook determine the way we dress. In England we were wearing big overcoats with hoods, and flat-heeled shoes: the feeling behind them being that we could walk, if there was no transport, and wrap up in our coat somewhere if we couldn't get home. We wanted to be ready for anything that was asked of us. Paris was in a totally different situation. Occupied by the Germans, its people wanted to cock a snook at them, distancing themselves by being flagrantly unpractical and putting on the most outrageous fashion show they could. So, with no transport but bicycles and a limited Métro service, they were wearing shoes with platform soles inches high, and towering hats.

I was installed in a splendour never enjoyed before or since. I had a two-room suite at the Ritz, furnished in blue and silver brocade; but food was so scarce that Bettina Ballard, an American fashion editor formerly based in Paris and just returned, bought me a bag of buns to take into the Ritz restaurant. One of the famous tea-rooms of Paris had been turned into a Services canteen, and I was given a pass to allow me to eat there. One night I dined with American journalist friends in the Hôtel Scribe, which had become their headquarters. Those serving the meal had seized on the belief that Americans liked coffee, so this was brought before the soup and at intervals throughout the meal. The only coffee available was made from acorns, but it would have been offensive to refuse what the French had had to put up with for years, though its bitterness made it hard to swallow.

I had brought with me a map of Paris and, whenever I stopped to look at it, passers-by gathered round me to find their way. They were mainly French, but from other parts of the country. The Métro was working, but so many stations were closed that the train kept flashing past my chosen station and I had to get out in an unknown area and find my way back on foot. Another trap for the unwary was the electricity control programme. The Government had decreed that there should be an hour's power cut every other hour throughout the day. It was supposed to fall on the hour but was not reliable, so I would stand in front of one of those small, shaky lifts, looking at my watch, and wondering whether I should reach the high upper floor in time or get stuck half-way for an hour.

Yet all these minor trials counted for nothing against the mere fact of being in Paris – and a Paris more beautiful than I shall ever see again. Just imagine the city with practically no traffic, only a few bicycles and an occasional army truck. One could cross the Champs-Elysées without bothering to look either way. The pavements were uncrowded. The September days were cloudless and still. When one walked along the Seine, the only movement one could see was that of a leaf dropping into the water.

Two years later, in the bitter winter of 1947/8, I was in Paris for the January collections and took myself off to the Louvre when they were over. Entering a long gallery I was surprised to see small groups of visitors, several yards apart, the members of each group standing closely together, gazing fixedly at the painting in front of them. Every now and again individuals, or a whole group, would move to the position formerly occupied by another group and would concentrate again on a single painting. I couldn't imagine what was so special about those particular pictures, and why all the ones between were passed by without a glance. But I soon found out. Each group was standing on the grille of a heating system through which hot air flowed.

Besides making contact with our colleagues in Paris, one purpose of my visit was to find, and bring back with me, a promising fashion artist. In London we were desperately short of artists and photographers. We were planning to run a competition to attract photographers, but Paris was thought of as a source of fashion artists and Michel de Brunhoff produced several for me to meet. I picked one, who was to return with me. He spoke no English, and naturally, on account of the war, he had never been out of France. Our cross-Channel journey was no encouragement. It was horribly rough and I forbore to translate the announcement that the usual distribution of life-jackets would not be made, as conditions were 'unsuitable'. The boat was packed and included a group of nuns, who staggered about the decks, hampered by their flowing garments. I tried to assist one who needed to reach the side in order to vomit, and inappropriately addressed her as 'Madame'. In Paris I was amused that when my young artist companion had given his address in Versailles and said it was his father's 'hôtel', I had guessed, correctly, that that confusing word referred to the home of a rather distinguished family, whereas Michel had taken it that his father was an *hôtelier*.

The New Look that Christian Dior launched later was the kick-start which fashion needed to make the transition from war to peace. Simply by its use of enormous quantities of fabric, it was the antithesis of the utility scheme clothes that were so suitable in wartime. Hardy Amies made me a beautiful dress in grey wool with a finely pleated skirt so voluminous and long that I had to pick it up with my hands when climbing stairs – a gesture I had not seen since observing grown-ups as a child before the 1914–18 war. But modern life makes its own demands, and it was impossible to wear it on a bus. Mostly I got my clothes from the ready-to-wear firms who showed their collections to the press well in advance. London had greatly benefited by the exodus from Nazi Germany and Austria of several outstanding manufacturers, who transformed our fashion scene. It was wonderful to be able to earmark something that would simply turn up a few months later. I never enjoyed shopping; and for years had no need to shop, except for shoes.

It took a while for life-styles to become international. I was in Rome in the summer of 1947, and so was a colleague from French *Vogue*. Each of us had brought the very similar, formal clothes we should have worn in our own cities – and they were hopelessly wrong. Romans were dressing, not for a city but for a resort. The streets were full of beautiful young women, all hatless, in sleeveless, pale-coloured linen dresses, bare legs and sandals. A fashion editor, who had known Rome before the war, said many belonged to families whose daughters would previously not have set foot in the streets but would have been taken everywhere by car. Returning home via Stresa I had the hilarious experience of being roped in to judge a *Concorso dei bambini belli*: not exactly a baby show, as the age limit was five. Italian mothers being the proudest in existence, the competitive atmosphere was tense, and angry cries went up when a doctor on the panel – who examined the children's teeth as if they were horses – pronounced them to be over-age. We made ourselves unpopular by awarding the prize to an exquisite Milanese visitor instead of a native infant.

Even before the war ended we at *Vogue* had felt sufficiently confident to plan for post-war publishing. Harry Yoxall felt that it was time to launch the British edition of another magazine from Condé Nast's New York stable. We settled on *House & Garden*; and then had all the stress and excitement of launching it on the public. It needed its hand held for only a few months and then steamed ahead with increasing success.

My visit to Paris had been strange and thrilling, but I was seeing European colleagues with whom we had shared wartime experiences, different though these were. Three months later, however, I was to make a stranger and even more thrilling journey, to establish links with our parent company in New York. There were no transatlantic flights by civil airlines in those days, and every passenger ship was crowded with American servicemen, eager for repatriation. So I was booked to travel by flying boat. There were three of these in service, and mine was the one used by Winston Churchill for such journeys as visiting troops in North Africa before the Battle of Alamein. I think there were about twenty passengers, of whom three were women, and a large cabin at the rear had been divided into cubicles for our use.

In mid-December we took off from Poole on the first leg of our flight, to Lisbon. The interior of the aircraft was so spacious that we were not confined to particular seats but could stroll about like guests in a hotel lounge. Meals were served in a separate section, and when we were given the signal we got up and went to the dining area, where we were astonished to find tropical fruit we had not seen for five years. We flew so low that we could always see land or sea and follow the contour of the dividing line between them. There were only two snags. One was that our anchorage was to a hook in the water that became invisible after dusk, which meant that we had to arrive at each destination in daylight. The other snag was the official fear of tropical diseases being carried by travellers like us who were in Europe one day, Africa the next, then Latin America, the Caribbean, and finally the United States. So when it was decreed that we should dock for some hours, with passengers going ashore (as happened at Lagos), a launch arrived with a doctor and his assistants. They systematically sprayed us and the whole interior with some chemical, and left us hermetically sealed (the outside temperature was 110 degrees) until any bugs were dead. We were then removed, dripping with sweat, and taken to a pleasant little hotel, where we threw ourselves into baths.

I had always wanted to visit Latin America, so it was wonderful that we spent our only night on the ground in Belem, Brazil. I had never been to Portugal, so the houses, typically colour-washed green, blue, pink and yellow, were a surprise and a delight. The other women passengers stayed in the hotel and enjoyed its hairdressing facilities, while the men went shopping for gifts for their wives or girl-friends. They rather went over the top, and returned with leather goods made repulsive, to me, by crocodile paws. I was determined to use the few hours of daylight to see what I might never see again: a Latin-American town. So, in my winter clothes and walking shoes – the original mad dog and Englishwoman – I strolled among the inhabitants of Belem, all dressed in cottons and sandals. There were avenues of flowering jacaranda trees, and the church interiors were ornate to an extent beyond anything I had ever seen. That evening our communal dinner was made merrier by the discovery that all the huge door keys we had been given, as if for the portcullis to a medieval castle, were identical.

Next morning we took off and flew for what seemed like hours over the delta of the Amazon. Its reddish soil stretched out endlessly, partly covered by the straggling greenery of trees and intersected by innumerable streams. The force of the Amazon carried its red water far out to sea, before it merged with the blue-green of the Atlantic. Free from the coast of Brazil we passed over that notorious French penal colony, Devil's Island, where Dreyfus had been held, and landed at Trinidad, whose woods appeared dense enough to rest upon, as on a cushion. When briefly we were on shore, the black women, in their bright clothes and headscarves tied to stand up like rabbits' ears, looked wildly exotic after the drab surroundings of our past years. Our low flight-level gave us a marvellous view of the Caribbean, the contours of its islands cut out as sharply as with scissors, and the sea breaking on their rocks and reefs. On the fifth day of our flight we arrived at Boston and took trains to our various destinations. Mine was New York.

I had been there only once before, in 1938, when I was an unknown quantity to my American colleagues. London was a junior partner in those days, and I a comparative junior in it. Then I had hovered by the open door of the editor, Mrs Chase, and was waved away until the day before my departure, when I was told to come in and shut the door so that we could talk. The London pattern department had given me a difficult task. Our famous paper patterns were all designed in the United States and imported into England, but our countries were not always wearing the same clothes – particularly lingerie. In England, in the thirties, camiknickers were a favourite undergarment: they were a kind of loose vest, with an extending back-piece that passed between one's legs and buttoned on at the front. Many women who did not feel up to tackling a dress or coat enjoyed making lingerie for themselves, and as presents to friends, so I had been instructed to persuade our American colleagues to introduce camiknicker patterns into the range. I made an appointment with the head of pattern design, described the garment and produced a specimen. It was handled sceptically and rejected out of hand, with the words, 'In America, we wouldn't have that much time.'

Now, seven years later, I was in New York again in very different circumstances. With a victorious end to the war the British were popular. I represented British *Vogue* and, momentarily, Britain itself. Our New York colleagues had been immensely generous in sending food parcels to us, and I had thanks to convey. So it was a happy atmosphere. Life in New York had been untouched by war, and therefore seemed to me as splendid and unreal as a pantomime. Huge lighted Christmas trees ran the whole length of Park Avenue. The costume jewellery counters at Saks seemed a hundred yards long. Waiting at a bus-stop one afternoon I saw a real-life New Yorker cartoon subject: a couple trying to hail a taxi after Christmas shopping – the opulent wife in furs, carrying only a handbag, while her smaller husband held a pile of parcels that reached up to his chin.

Colleagues entertained me lavishly. At one lunch party the other guests were Marlene Dietrich and Salvador Dali. I was asked to name people I should like to meet at a cocktail party, and chose the cartoonists Saul Steinberg and Charles Addams.

The Addams family were already celebrities about whom stories were told. One was of a cartoon that even *The New Yorker* had felt it impossible to publish. The scene was a maternity ward, which 'Mrs Addams' was about to leave with a bundle in her arms. The nurse's words made the caption: 'Shall I wrap it for you, madam – or will you eat it here?' Steinberg's cartoon-men were self-portrait caricatures, always utterly expressionless. Two impecunious young theatrical producers, whom I knew slightly in London, were planning to stage Menotti's *The Medium* and had persuaded Steinberg to design the backdrop. Only after he left did they realize that they had never fixed a fee, so they followed him to Paris and put the question, nervously. He said, 'I suggest that you name a figure, and if my face shows any sign of emotion, it's too little.'

Edna Chase, editor of American *Vogue* for some fifty years, and who, together with its publisher, Condé Nast, had invented and developed the magazine, was a remarkable woman – not only for that achievement but because, while taking enormous pride in her creation and total control of its running, she had managed to remain a simple human being, with feet firmly on the ground. Typically, before I even left the hotel on my first morning, she was on the telephone. 'I don't suppose you thought of bringing galoshes with you, dear? Well, it's snowing here, and you'll need them. Give me your shoe size, and I'll have a pair waiting for you.' I was in her office one day when she made a call to a firm from whose advertisement she had ordered a slip. It was too long; she asked to change it for one of the same bust size but shorter, and was told that there was only one length and she had better turn it up. 'Put me through to your manager,' she said, and then she let fly – not on personal grounds but with righteous indignation that any *Vogue* reader should get such pitiful service from a *Vogue* advertiser. At least three lengths for every bust size were needed, and I had no doubt that, from then on, three lengths there would be.

I sat in on a discussion about the main theme of the fashion pages in a spring issue. The fashion editor and her staff said that the leading colour story was of the palest possible cream-beige. They wanted sixteen pages devoted to it, covering coats, suits and dresses. Edna listened quietly; it seemed settled; they got up to leave. Then she said, 'Have you thought of the cleaning bills, dears? And a woman wants something she can wear, not something that's always at the cleaners.' So they sat down again and thought it over, and settled for eight pages of beige and eight of navy blue.

I left the United States on New Year's Eve 1945/6, taking the same flying boat from Boston. This time our numbers were greatly reduced to five or six men, and me. While the outward flight had taken five days, the return needed only three, on account of the prevailing winds, which greatly affected our low-flying craft. But a tropical storm blew up and we were forced to spend the night in Bermuda. After a twenty-four-hour flight we arrived in Lisbon. Could we then be refuelled in time to reach Poole in daylight? We stood by while men hand-pumped away. But it was no use, and we were told to go away and amuse ourselves until three o'clock the following morning. The reprieve suited us well, for none of us knew Lisbon. Of course there was no point in going to bed, so we were picked up from a night-club and driven to the dock. In the dark, with a rough sea rocking the floating walkway leading to our craft, an imaginative tourist board presented each of us with a pineapple and a bottle of port.

The first sensation of the post-war period was the general election which brought Labour into power. Other countries – and especially the United States – could not believe that we had rejected Churchill, who had been a supreme leader throughout a war which ended in victory. I regarded it as a result which showed that the British electorate had come of age and was able to judge that the right leader in war might not be the right leader in peace. I was delighted by the result of that general election, as I had voted Labour since I cast my first vote in the late 1920s.

In New York, in the winter of 1945, I encountered American disgust at the Labour victory when I lunched with one of *Vogue*'s most important advertisers, Elizabeth Arden. Miss Arden flew at me with 'You people must have been out of your minds to let those Labourites in! You've got to get rid of them right away!' To which I replied as politely as possible that the British system was for five-year terms and that, towards the end of this period, there would be another general election at which the electorate would make its choice again. If she had known that I had helped to vote the 'Labourites' in, I think she would have cancelled her advertising in British *Vogue*. Hers was not a character that appealed to me, whereas that of her arch-rival, Helena Rubinstein, did. On one of Madame Rubinstein's visits to London, I and other editors were invited to tea at her hotel. She was accompanied everywhere by a young Irishman who acted as her secretary and general factotum; so, when she described a painting she had bought in Paris, she said, 'Show it to the ladies, Patrick', and he put his hand into his breast pocket and produced a painting the size of a postcard. It was by a well-known artist, Jean Hugo, and showed an expanse of snow with a tiny troika approaching the edge of a forest. She had bought it as a gift for her husband, one of the numerous Georgian princes beloved of wealthy Americans. Madame Rubinstein, who certainly fell into that category, told us what she had paid for it, and thought it was a large price for something so small. 'But then,' she said, 'I thought – it's for the Prince.' There was something touching in this powerful, self-made woman confiding her doubts to a group of strangers, so I took pleasure in a story that highlighted the bitterness of the Rubinstein/Arden cosmetics war. Miss Arden had a racing stable in which she took great interest, and one day the papers carried a report which a colleague read out to Helena Rubinstein. 'Oh, Madame. Miss Arden has been bitten by one of her horses!' 'Really?' was the reply. 'And how is the horse?'

The sinister McCarthy hearings, which decimated the creative and intellectual sections of American society by hunting down left-wing opinion (labelled communism), had a spin-off that hit me. Visas were needed for all entries into the United States, and the day before I was due to fly to New York every existing visa was revoked overnight. A phone call to the US Embassy confirmed that I – like everyone else – must come to the Embassy to renew my visa. Its hall resembled an enlargement of the scene of Menotti's *The Consul*, in which the characters endlessly and hopelessly apply for visas. It was a pandemonium of frantic people. Visas were granted only to those who had received them from the Embassy itself. Others had to go back to the consulate that had granted them – and this was often in some continental country. Whole families had sold everything before emigration and had nowhere to live. The cries and tears and despair were heart-rending. It was incredible that a great nation should fall victim to such an attack of meaningless hysteria, because all that was required for a new visa was to raise one's arm and swear that one was not, and never had been, a member of the Communist Party – and who would not be prepared to do that, in the search for a new life?

I never talked politics at the office but somehow my Labour leanings became known. They were mildly disapproved of by my own board but caused some alarm in New York, where I gathered it was unwise for anyone to be known as a Democrat. Condé Nast himself was such a hard-line Republican that he threatened to throw himself out of the eighteenth-floor window of the office above Grand Central Station if Roosevelt got a second term. He did; Condé didn't. But when I came back from the press conference at which Aneurin Bevan outlined his plans for a National Health Service, and I proposed to publish a piece on it, my fellow-directors said with one voice that it was quite outside the borders of the magazine's interests. Perhaps they were right. But *Vogue* did admit the existence of a Labour government by publishing a profile of Aneurin Bevan by Harold Nicolson, and a profile of the Foreign Secretary, Ernest Bevin, by the editor of the *New Statesman*, Kingsley Martin. Though left-wing, I never even flirted with communism – in fact I disliked it. So when (after I had long since retired) a newspaper, listing past editors of *Vogue* on the accession of a new one, described me as a Communist, I insisted on a retraction.

The most interesting of my brief visits to Buckingham Palace occurred during the war. We had been told that the Queen had commissioned John Piper to make a series of drawings of Windsor Castle, that these were temporarily at the Palace, and that we could photograph two or three of them for publication. I think we had been alerted because, earlier in the war, we had had the Queen's permission to publish a beautiful drawing Augustus John had made of her – the preliminary sketch for a portrait which, unfortunately, never materialized. Hearing of the Pipers, a photographer, the art editor and I set out to see them and were directed to the side entrance, near the Royal Mews. From there we were escorted down a flight of stairs to the basement – but a basement transformed into a VIP bomb shelter. Off the corridor, all the way along, there was a series of tiny rooms – bedrooms, living-rooms, a dining-room, exquisitely furnished to scale with treasures from the V & A. Between every few rooms there was a massive bomb-proof door.

Later I heard a story which I hope is not apocryphal. John Piper was well known for the stormy settings to his landscapes. Osbert Sitwell describes settling him to sketch, one radiant morning, on the terrace of the family home, Renishaw Hall, but thunder-clouds gathered immediately – 'Nature imitating art'. The story went that, when the drawings reached Windsor, the Queen and the artist were looking at the display when the King walked in unexpectedly. She introduced them, saying, 'Do look at these beautiful drawings which Mr Piper has made for us.' He duly did; but his only comment was 'Shocking luck with the weather, Mr Piper.'

During the present reign, members of the Design Council were invited to Buckingham Palace for tea in a first-floor sitting-room overlooking the garden which, since I had never been to a royal garden party, surprised me by its size. In the course of conversation the Duke of Edinburgh remarked that he had recently attended an exhibition where there was some work by Picasso – and the fellow couldn't even draw. Forgetting where I was, I chipped in with, 'He can draw very well. It's just that he prefers to draw like that.' This was received with stunned silence.

Lord Snowdon earned admiration and respect for the discreet handling of his divorce, but I had an advance sample of those skills at an earlier date, when he was plain Tony Armstrong-Jones, *Vogue* photographer. At that period all our photographers were under contract and Tony's was running out at the end of the year. I asked him to discuss it, but he was always too busy and could assure me only that he wouldn't work for anyone else. I was in Paris for the January collections when the French *Vogue* office called me up to ask whether they could give my telephone number to the press. 'Whatever do they want?' 'Don't you know?

It's just been announced that Tony Armstrong-Jones is engaged to Princess Margaret.' I didn't know. No one knew. Thankful that I was staying with a sister-in-law rather than at our usual berth, the Crillon, I escaped the press but found a back-street post office, whose staff I electrified by sending a telegram of congratulation to Buckingham Palace, which had taken Tony in, for protection.

It is strange that the royal box at Covent Garden should not have been placed in the obvious central position; so this has to be created for special occasions. On one of these, for the visit of the French president, I was given a private view by the director, David Webster, of the exquisite confection conjured up by Oliver Messel. He also took me on a tour of the permanent royal box, which has an ante-room where drinks are served in the intervals, and a loo so discreet that it quietly flushes itself as the door is closed. When, as part of the coronation celebrations, Britten's *Gloriana* was given a first performance, the audience was as spectacular as the stage. Probably for the last time in the theatre's history everyone was in full evening dress, and as the lights were lowered, the diamond tiaras and necklaces flashed their brilliance in a positive firework display.

A very different experience of Covent Garden was on an ocasion when I took Edna Chase to a performance of *Billy Budd*. Benjamin Britten was a post-war celebrity; our New York visitors always wanted to see London's most talked-of shows; *Billy Budd* was newly presented, so I did the honours. I was aware that my guest was less than enthusiastic, and, in the taxi to her hotel she said, 'Thank you, my dear. I have to say that was not my idea of opera. I think of opera as showing charming people in beautiful clothes, and having tunes which one can hum.' There was no doubt that *Billy Budd* did not fit that description.

The post-war years saw a surge of activity in British commercial life. The cost of the war had brought the economy to ruins. It was essential that we should improve our export trade. *Vogue* played an important part in setting up a London equivalent of the Paris couture, under the title of the Incorporated Society of London Fashion Designers. Of the ten firms forming the group, the leading designers of their day, only one survives: that of

Hardy Amies. Sir Hardy attributes his success to two things: that the women's side of his business remains truly 'bespoke', his designs being adapted by first-class fitters to suit individual customers; and that his men's ready-to-wear tailoring is marketed under licence around the globe, with a growing demand in the Far East. I would add a third reason: his business expertise – rarely found in creative people. The members of the Incorporated Society showed their collections shortly before Paris, so that buyers and journalists could cover both events in sequence. It had influential presidents in Lady Pamela Berry (as she then was), wife of the proprietor and editor of the *Daily Telegraph*, and Lady Rothermere. But London's ready-to-wear output was of such high quality, and *haute couture* was so expensive, that the group broke up, and individual firms went out one by one, over the years.

Another venture of the post-war period flourishes to this day. It was realized that, as a country, Britain was backward in design, and the Council for Industrial Design (now shortened to the Design Council) was set up by the Government, with Gordon Russell as its director. I had the privilege and pleasure of being a member of that Council. Privilege, because it is always exciting to be in at the birth of a development; and pleasure, because Gordon was the only director with whom I have worked in such a capacity who really took his Council into his confidence. He consulted us, listened to us, argued with us, and altogether made us feel as if we were a useful part of the enterprise. The Council members represented leading firms in important lines of business; and not by any means all of them were in sympathy with the Council's aims; but Gordon handled our meetings with such charm, tact and humour that no one showed actual antagonism.

In 1947 Gordon assigned me to work with a group consisting of representatives of firms from the cutlery manufacturers of Sheffield and the china manufacturers of the Potteries. We met in the Goldsmiths' Hall in the City. It had been damaged in the bombing and there was no central heating; it was a bitter winter; even the men kept on their overcoats and hats. We didn't seem to be getting anywhere, and I told Gordon how gloomy I felt. 'Try to remember,' he said, 'that it is an achievement just to get them sitting round the same table.' I don't know how things are now, but then industries were incredibly isolated from one another and from reality. One Sheffield firm, for instance, made only carving forks; none of its design staff ever saw a carving knife. One enterprising cutlery firm director on our committee said that he sometimes hired a coach to take staff to visit firms in the Potteries. 'What's the point of that?' demanded another; and it had to be explained that, when a table was laid for dinner, knives and forks would be set each side of a place, and then a plate would be put down in the middle, and it was interesting to consider the design relationship between the two. It was uphill work.

In 1952, the year before the coronation, the Design Council decided to take a hand in the design of coronation souvenirs. I was given the chairmanship of a large committee composed of distinguished independent designers and representatives of firms with a high design reputation whose products were not in the souvenir category. We sat frequently, over many months, and we tried not merely to accept or reject but to help firms to improve their products by suggesting changes in material, in colouring, in lettering. They would then be submitted again and might be accepted, which would give them the right to carry the Council's stamp of approval. I think our work was useful, and that it helped to produce some good-looking souvenirs.

It was to boost the young Council's image that, on account of this job, my name was put forward for a small gong – also considered as a tribute to the whole group of women's magazines, which had been giving extensive coverage to the events of coronation year. As my divorce was listed at that point, and royalty never met divorcees (they were barred from the royal enclosure at Ascot), it was felt that I should report this to the honours list secretary at 10 Downing Street. He assumed, incorrectly, that I was divorcing my husband, but took heart from the fact that I worked under my maiden name, and said that the matter would be referred to the Queen. I hope that they never bothered her with anything so trivial, but the official message was that she wished me to accept the honour.

I had worked on a panel of judges assessing fashion design for competitions sponsored by the Royal Society of Arts, the whole of whose title, 'for the encouragement of Arts, Manufactures and Commerce', is often overlooked by the public but not by the Society itself. I was appointed to the Council in my first year of retirement, but was so disabled by a spine operation that I could not attend the required number of meetings and beat a rather ignominious retreat. But I still have the handsome Bicentenary Medal which they present each year 'For Services to Industrial Art'; and which they gave me when I left *Vogue*.

5

Victor and I met in the most unlikely way. In the early summer of 1938 I was sent to New York to meet our colleagues. My husband Jock naturally wanted to visit America, so he was to join me after my month at the office, and we were to go on a round trip of the United States. A few days after Jock's arrival, a man approached us in a street in Manhattan. He and Jock greeted each other. The man was Victor, a Russian émigré who had changed his name from Kraminsky to Kennett. He had shared a cabin with Jock on the voyage from Southampton. We told him that we were going that evening to the Rainbow Room and asked him to join us. We were returning on the wonderful new French liner, the *Normandie*. Victor told me later that he went to a travel agent the next day and booked his passage on the same voyage.

Jock and I made an amazing train journey which gave us a better idea of the United States than many Americans possess, and which travelling by air could never provide. From Chicago we took the southernmost transcontinental route through Kansas, New Mexico and Arizona to Los Angeles. Even on the train we saw America's prohibition laws in action. Near us in the lounge car sat an elderly woman quietly playing patience. As we crossed the border into Kansas a guard took away her cards, locking them in a wall cupboard. Two hours later, as we crossed into New Mexico, he unlocked the cupboard and gave her cards back: Kansas was a 'no-gambling state'.

We found Los Angeles boring. It seemed to have no heart, but just to go on and on. San Francisco was a different story; it is surely among the most thrilling cities in the world. From there we had a weekend in Yosemite. A waterfall called the Bridal Veil falls from such a height that the water disintegrates into droplets before reaching the valley floor. One night, men whom one was then allowed to call Red Indians built a huge bonfire on the cliff, and pushed the blazing faggots over the edge to make a fire-fall. Very spectacular. From San Francisco we went on to Portland, then turned the corner and travelled through the Rockies, North and South Dakota, the rich farmland of Minnesota, and back to Chicago. We had circled America, enjoying wide views of the country from the windows of the lounge cars, and watching the landscape rushing away from us as we stood on the platform jutting out from the last coach.

When, after our return, we were boarding the *Normandie*, there was Victor, who had ordered the largest possible bouquet to be delivered to our cabin. As the ship rolled one night the vase of flowers fell on us and we were soaked. I learnt later that Jock had suggested to Victor that he should keep me amused while he amused himself elsewhere. Victor and his wife were separated at that point. He could have drawn conclusions from Jock's remark, but he needed no encouragement. He had already made up his mind to get me to leave Jock and join him. He had this extraordinary confidence from the moment we met that we should be together. I was attracted to him, but I didn't feel the same confidence. In those days divorce was a very serious step.

While spending a weekend with my parents, my father sensed something disturbing and was appalled at the news. He said that a love affair on a voyage was a silly novelettish thing on which such a step could not possibly be based. He was the main influence in my life and I cared for his approval before all else. In London I went into a hotel to think it out, and was bombarded with letters from Victor as well as from Jock, who implored me to stay with him. Later I realized that Jock was desperate at the thought of supporting his parents alone. Finally I told Victor that I wouldn't come to him.

Thirteen years went by and my marriage had ceased to exist, though I made sure that no one had the slightest idea of its failure. Jock and I were good friends. We shared tastes in music, theatre, art and books. People who liked us at all liked us both. But he was never without a girl-friend. When a husband told me that he was taking divorce proceedings, naming Jock as co-respondent (and he supposed I would do the same), I said that Jock could have a divorce when he wanted it, but so far he hadn't. Of course if there had been nothing else in my life, it would have been unbearable. But how seldom does anyone have everything? And if something is missing, the gap can be filled with something else, which, for me, was absorbing work – probably too absorbing for the good of a marriage, especially to a husband who disliked work and longed only to retire.

One day Victor rang me in my office from the north of England. He was coming to London and asked me to meet him. I thought there could be nothing left between us after all those years; and, in any case, I had no marriage to save. So we met, and it was just as if we had never parted. This was in 1951. Victor was desperate. He had gone back to his wife after my decision in 1938, but with no success. He told me how it ended. His wife persuaded him that he was mentally unstable and got him into a hospital for nervous diseases. She then went abroad. He was put to bed in a single room, and his clothes were taken away. For two or three weeks he was under supervision, constantly interrogated. Finally a doctor came in and said, 'There is nothing whatever the matter with you. I am sending your clothes in. Put them on and get out of here.' It was at this point that Victor rang me up.

His work was in the north, and the only place in London where we could stay was a hotel. This had its problems. One hotel somehow discovered that we were not married and refused to accept a second booking. When we decided we must give our spouses grounds for divorce, we gave the address of a hotel in Woodstock, where we had spent a weekend. The management was outraged, and said we could never stay there again. If divorce was a serious undertaking in 1938, that was still the case in 1951. There had to be guilty and innocent parties, and the 'innocent' on one side could sue for damages from the 'guilty' on the other: something Jock actually threatened to do. But before we reached that point Victor threw up his job in the north and we found a flat in Kensington. I had still not left Jock, and spent my time between Ennismore Gardens and Blomfield Road.

All was set for the final break when, one evening, I arrived home to find a telegram addressed to Stewart, which announced the death of a woman in Switzerland. From the arrival of letters with Swiss stamps I had guessed that Jock was attached to someone who needed to be there, and had presumed tuberculosis, because foreign currency was available only for urgent reasons. I sensed that this was a serious relationship, and Jock's grief at the news made it certain. I told Victor that I could not possibly leave him in such distress. And this was when Victor showed a true nobility of character. He had remembered me for thirteen years. He had at last persuaded me to join him. He had thrown up a highly paid job in the north to take a London flat where he had been living alone, with the precarious task of setting up a new business. And just when I was coming to him, I drew back. He was, by nature, the most impatient man alive; but at this point he became an example of that wonderful passage in *As You Like It*, which describes what it means to be in love: to be 'all patience and impatience'. He never said a word of reproach or self-pity, and a few weeks later I felt able to leave Jock and join him in Ennismore Gardens.

It was then that I experienced responses to my move which made me wonder whether simple, spontaneous reactions might not be the victims of higher education. I was short of good-luck wishes from the closest friends; but my daily, and Victor's, showed instant warm feeling. Mine asked to come with me. I had to explain that I could not displace Victor's devoted helper, and asked her to stay with Jock, which she did. Victor's daily had seen me come and go, and I was nervous about her reaction, as she was Irish and Catholic. But when I told her I had come to live, she cried, 'I'm so glad! Poor Mr Kennett! He's been so lonely.' And she stayed with us for twenty years.

A marriage is between not only two people but two families. Victor's family was dispersed – a brother and sister in the USSR, sisters in Paris, and a son working in India. I did not meet the Russian relatives till our first visit, six years later. His sisters I met on my twice-yearly attendances at the Paris collections and, after we retired, on frequent visits. They and their mother had left Russia in the early 1920s, when there was famine in the land and Lenin had pronounced that anyone not contributing to the economy could leave the country. They were then barely out of their teens. The elder, Lorka, went to the Sorbonne, and very soon she and her sister Alka married Ukrainian cousins. Lorka's husband was an outstanding engineer; the testing of his design of a new gun was attended by high-ranking officers, who invited him to work with the army – on condition that he applied for French citizenship. 'Never,' he replied. 'I shall return to Russia when the Tsar is once more on the throne.' And, following his example, Lorka remained stateless all her life. He insisted that she left the Sorbonne when they married, so, when she was widowed, she had no university degree. She was an excellent teacher of the Russian language, but without French citizenship could have only private pupils.

Victor's youngest sister, Alka, came to our rescue on several occasions, when one of us was ill. Her life, too, had been stunted by her husband. She was working in the drawing office of an engineering firm when they were married, but he made her give it up. He was the brilliant chief engineer of Sud-Aviation, which built the famous Caravelle; and Concorde was in production when he retired. He went to work early, returned late, and spent weekends translating new Russian publications for the benefit of his colleagues. There was not much time left for companionship.

I found it strange, and sad, that those two husbands had deliberately cramped the lives of the women they had married. Higher education for women was well known in pre-revolutionary Russia. There would have been plenty of scope for their wives to do interesting work in Paris. It was painful to hear Alka say that she envied me for having made something of my life. How could intelligent men suppose that intelligent women could find enough to occupy, let alone satisfy, them in a small flat, with only two people to shop and cook for?

When Victor arrived in Switzerland after his escape from the USSR his only contact was with the Handl family, whose daughters were his cousins through a Russian-Swiss marriage. Victor married the elder daughter, so the younger became his sister-in-law. She was later to become well known as the actress Irene Handl. Hers was a world of black and white, and she took the ending of her sister's marriage very hard. Their father, who was fond of Victor and visited us surreptitiously, described Irene's stance as that of being 'plus royaliste que le roi'. She maintained it until after her sister's death; and then her old affection for Victor returned and, in the last months when I left him only to do shopping, she came to sit with him. It surprised me that, after he died, she treated me as a friend.

I always had a sense of insecurity in the relationship, because Irene's reactions were so passionate and so unpredictable. She often lamented, with good reason, that she had become type-cast as a Cockney character, when she had the ability to take on a much wider range of roles. On one such occasion I ventured to suggest the part of the Nurse in *Romeo and Juliet*, to which she exclaimed, 'Good God, Audrey – Shakespeare!' Mention of a concert brought 'What kind of a concert? Chamber music! How awful!' And she told me that her father had left his native Vienna to get away from the music. When she was on *Desert Island Discs* all her eight chosen records were of Elvis Presley. Her powerful prejudices made her as loyal a friend as she was ruthless as an enemy. Towards the end of her life she sometimes forgot who I was, and talked to me about her sister's unhappy marriage, a topic in which I could take no part.

I don't know whether it is a Russian trait, or special to Victor's family, but I was constantly astonished by the implacable decisions they made about personal relationships. 'I will never speak to her again'; 'That's the last time I will ever do anything for him.' And they meant it. Even Victor sometimes spoke like that and, if I protested, would say, 'Well, you carry on if you want to.' But he said more than once that he was learning tolerance – and I think it made him happier. I let fly only once with Lorka, a religious woman, when she verbally struck some harmless person off her visiting list, and I found myself saying that it was a good thing that God took a more lenient view of our shortcomings.

On my side the only relative was my sister Monica, a remarkable character who had made a life for herself, unaided. When she retired as HM Inspector of Schools she made astonishing journeys, quite alone. After lecturing to a teachers' summer school in Los Angeles she made an on-the-spot decision to return via the Middle East and, without any reservations or currency, travelled through Iraq and Iran, Syria and Jordan, sharing taxis with Arabs across intervening deserts. When her United Nations group felt they needed to know more about their project in Botswana, Monica, in her seventies, volunteered to find out. While in Africa she was told that there was no means of knowing even on what day a train might appear: a problem she solved in the simplest manner possible – by camping on the station platform till it came.

The relationship between Victor and Monica was charming but comical for, to her, he was as strange a being as if he had dropped from Mars. She was sometimes baffled to exasperation and, the gentlest of people, would seize him by the shoulders and shake him – which he endured with great good humour. It felt strange to me, standing between these two and understanding them both, while they had little understanding of one another. In the last months of Victor's life I could no longer manage this tripartite relationship. Monica, always wanting to help, came to stay with us more and more frequently. Victor was suffering from angina pectoris, and suffering was the word. The slightest thing could bring on an attack: sometimes a physical movement but also any emotional disturbance. He also loved to be loved, and needed it to be shown. Monica had lived an entirely sexless life. She spoke only once of having loved a man and, when he did not respond, she had never loved again. I suppose it was what the psychologists call 'sublimation', which transformed the deprivation of sex into her wide-reaching love of mankind. When an old friend settled near her home in Saffron Walden, he wrote of her: 'She is so full of goodness. She radiates virtue like the sun.' But she could not watch any love scene on TV, however discreet; and, when she was present, I could not put my arms round Victor and murmur loving words. His needs, and mine, had to come first, so I told Monica as gently as I could that Victor and I must be alone as he ended his life. I am afraid she didn't understand. It was alien ground, on which she had never stood.

Victor was not one for looking back. If there was anything in the past that he regretted, he never spoke of it – except one thing. He never let me forget that I had kept him waiting for thirteen years. He regarded those as wasted years, being convinced that he had been deprived not only of happiness but of success. He constantly said that he needed a firm anchor; that he had felt all at sea; but that if I had been with him he would have had a successful business and made a lot of money. We could have done with a lot of money in later years, when we had a great weight of family responsibilities which could be met only by the sale of our collections of clocks and pictures; but wealth, in itself, had a curious attraction for him. He had two wealthy friends, and I didn't care for either of them – but they had a sort of mesmeric effect on Victor, which made him unable to see them as people but rather as symbols, whose life-style he envied.

His reproaches had to be endured in silence because I could not say that I regretted what I had done. In fact I felt that it had probably saved us from disaster. When we met I was managing editor of *Vogue*, and hoped to go higher in my profession. Victor would have been demanding, wanting me exclusively as his wife. Looking back, I realized that I was someone who needed a career, and that without some achievement of my own I should have felt frustrated and unfulfilled.

Children would have brought an additional problem. Victor was born in an authoritarian age, in an authoritarian country, of an authoritarian father. So it was natural for him to assume that he knew best. He was not prepared to accept that people did things in their own way. Often, when I was doing some manual job, he would take it out of my hands and show me how it should be done. This is a laughing matter in middle age; but it could be disastrous for a child – underminding its confidence, and discouraging it from making the endless experiments by which it learns about the world. I was brought up in an atmosphere of freedom, physical and mental; and it would be my instinct to leave a child to work things out for itself, unless that was really unwise. If we had had a family, we would have clashed on crucial matters of upbringing.

Victor was a born entrepreneur; probably not an ideal *employé*, but with the imagination and energy to see an opening and go for it. It was impossible to imagine him in a dole queue; he would always have come up with an idea – and the enterprise to carry it out. When the slump came in the late twenties and his son Fred was still a baby, he lost his job. He was a foreigner; and last in, first out. What he did was totally characteristic. He noticed that country houses were coming on to the market on account of new laws on Inheritance Tax, which often had to be paid by their sale. He was a keen photographer, so he went to the still-famous estate agents, Knight, Frank & Rutley, and put it to them that photographs of the contents of such houses would arouse interest, bring buyers. They agreed, but would commit themselves just to paying ten shillings for any print they chose. So he would set off by train, with his heavy studio camera on his back, get out at some remote station and walk several miles to the house concerned. His scheme was such a success that, in less than a year, he was employing two men to do the processing. But, one day, he saw an advertisement for an engineer and thought, well, that's my profession. So he applied for it, got it, and gave up photography – for the time being.

Very early in the war a warehouse in the north of England had been taken over by the Ministry of Defence for producing radar equipment, and Victor was put in charge of it. They not only made the equipment – and its secret was then known only in Britain – but fitted it into vans exactly like those of the army postal and telegraph service. One night in 1940, when the British Army in France was gathering at Dunkirk – waiting to be evacuated, as the Germans were driving them into the sea – a Ministry official rang up, telling him to send one of his senior colleagues to London immediately. He was to be briefed and then flown to France, to trace the radar vans. These had distinctive markings, recognizable only to those who had made them. Victor called up his chief engineer, who said that nothing would induce him to go, it was far too dangerous. So Victor got into his car and drove south through the night. He went to the Ministry, received his orders, was provided with a colonel's uniform, but with the warning, 'If you're captured by the Germans they will never believe that you're a British officer and will probably shoot you.' He was then flown to Dunkirk, where he was given a small team of sappers whose job was to blow up each van as it was identified. There were eighty vans to be traced and Victor found seventy-eight of them. The search had to end; the situation was getting very tense, and he was flown back. He went straight to the Ministry. The officer in charge said that he had done extremely well, and he was given the Freedom of the City of London.

This episode illustrates the instinctive, unselfconscious courage that Victor possessed, by which I mean that he did not need to nerve himself to do a brave thing; he simply did it. It was a quality as natural to him as breathing, and it is clear that in the early days of the Russian Revolution his family turned to him automatically in every crisis. His young sister's school had been evacuated to the Caucasus, which was coming under threat from a German invasion, so Victor set off on a forty-day rail journey to bring them all back. In the brief reminiscences made towards the end of his life he wrote: 'In a stretch of several thousand kilometres, everywhere we saw pilfering, arson, murder. At one station the White Guards, who consisted mainly of officers, were being executed by the Workers' Party, armed with rifles. It was a ghastly sight. At another station we saw workers and peasants executed by the officers.'

His next foray was to the distant Vologda region to rescue his brother, who was near death from the deadly influenza epidemic. He fed him with a broth made from a capercaillie – exchanged for tobacco – and walked 40 miles, there and back, to acquire 18 pounds of butter, unknown in Leningrad for a year. In the flat where he lived with his mother and young sisters they listened every day to 'incessant rifle fire, from the execution of people who were declared the enemies of the proletariat. It was horrible to hear it, knowing that with every shot a life was lost'. They were on starvation rations, even bread was scarce and heating oil unobtainable, so, when his brother heard that a barrel of kerosene could be had if they came late at night to a goods yard, they set off with their sleigh. But they had to smuggle it all the way back because, when they opened it at home, there was a body in the kerosene.

Victor's father, who was gravely ill with angina pectoris, and had been allowed to go to Switzerland for treatment, wrote that he was dying and wished to see one of his sons. The three drew lots, and it fell to Victor. On New Year's Eve 1918 he set out for the far north Finnish border, because the southern end was heavily guarded. For four days he dug himself into the snow during the day and walked through the night. He was nearly shot by Finnish soldiers on the border; had a slow and difficult journey to Switzerland; and three weeks after his arrival his father died. His first thought was to return to Leningrad, but the Red Cross bureau in Geneva told him he would be shot at once. This advice was confirmed years later by a contemporary of his, whose brothers were visiting Sweden when the Revolution broke out. Full of enthusiasm for its ideals, they rushed back – to be seized and shot.

So Victor became an exile for forty years. He seldom spoke about his escape. Nevertheless the trauma of setting out alone, in the dark and the snow, not knowing if he would get out alive or ever see his family again, made so deep an impression that the first weeks of each new year were always clouded, as he relived that perilous time. But he was a survivor, and would have been a marvellous companion in a potential disaster involving any of the elements – earth, fire, air or water.

To return to radar: if the two missing vans at Dunkirk were captured, their secrets were never discovered by the Germans, and Victor was such an acknowledged expert on radar that he was sent several times to the United States, to instruct American engineers in its manufacture. These journeys were very hazardous – sometimes made by flying in the bomb-racks of planes, sometimes travelling in naval convoys, which almost always saw one or more of their number blown up by a torpedo from an enemy submarine. His contacts were mostly in Chicago, for which he developed a positive affection which shocked Americans from more respectable cities.

I was always astonished at the passion for quality that Victor possessed. He went for the best just as a compass needle points to the north; and he was incapable of buying one of anything. An extraordinary episode arose from this multi-buying habit of his. At some point he had joined a textile manufacturer in the north of England. On a visit to a company making shirts from his firm's textiles he was invited to order anything he fancied, so went round marking two of this, three of that, not realizing that he was ordering them by the dozen. He wore a few from time to time, but piles remained unworn. Then came 1940, Hitler's invasion of the Low Countries and France, and a mass exodus from the Continent to Britain. Boatloads of refugees arrived, and the Lord Mayor of London made an appeal for clothing. Victor asked his secretary to send piles of shirts to the appeal, and he got a letter of thanks from the Lord Mayor. Some weeks later he was summoned to Scotland Yard and questioned about his connections with Holland. He had none. Did he know a certain Dutchman, now in England? He didn't. He was advised to think it over, then questioned again. He repeated that he didn't know the man. 'Then how,' they said, 'could he be wearing one of your shirts?' At first Victor was baffled, but then the only possible explanation came to him: 'I gave shirts to the Lord Mayor's Appeal.' 'How can you prove that?' 'I had a letter of thanks from the Lord Mayor.' 'Let us see it.' Victor feared it had been destroyed, but his secretary produced it. The police then explained that the man in question was a spy, and that when he was arrested his shirt had laundry marks traced to Victor's laundry, and his ownership.

Victor was a considerable expert on rugs and clocks. Our various homes happened to have good floor boards, so we never needed carpets but had a spread of beautiful rugs. We carried three to the families in Leningrad, laying them on the floor of the boot and covering them with a tarpaulin. But his chief passion was for clocks. I believe that, before my time, he had sixty. I remember Arnold Bennett describing a car drive in France when a woman passenger cried 'Stop!' as they drove through a town, because she had seen a hat in a shop window. Arnold Bennett remarked, 'What an eye she had for a hat!' Victor had an eye for a clock. He was driving through Richmond one late afternoon during the war when the air-raid siren went off. At that moment he saw a clock in a shop window and went in to look at it. The shopkeeper wanted to lock up and get home before any bombs fell. Victor began asking questions about the clock's mechanism, upon which it was pushed into his hands at an absurdly low price. 'Just take it, and get out,' he was told.

Since Victor was an engineer, it was the mechanism that was his primary interest. They were all regulator clocks, of the late eighteenth and early nineteenth century; some long case, some bracket clocks. Victor understood them as if they had been people. When, in our early days together, summer-time came round, I spoke of the long job it would be to change them all. 'I've done it already,' he said; and he had done it so swiftly that I hadn't noticed. My contribution was my parents' grandfather clock, which featured the stages of the moon. The famous firm of Frodsham, now extinct, was always brought in to pack the clocks when we moved house. They made fun of my old-fashioned piece, which was so tall that the only place for it in the farmhouse was the kitchen extension.

Whenever we were away from home Victor would arrange with Frodsham to call each week in order to wind the clocks. This caused a drama, which was described to us on our return from Peru to Gloucester Place Mews. Our neighbours had been burgled and were on the look-out for any dubious goings-on in the mews. They knew we were away, yet noticed that a man had ridden up on a bicycle and entered our house. As he did not reappear, they called the police, and two plain-clothes officers came round and rang the bell. They rang and rang, and when an elderly man finally appeared they shouted, 'Why the hell didn't you answer the bell sooner?' 'I am not here to answer the bell. One never knows who it may be, does one?' 'Well, what are you here for anyway?' 'I am here to wind Mr Kennett's clocks. I wind the clocks in Buckingham Palace.' H.M. Bateman, the cartoonist, might have captioned it, 'Collapse of stout party'.

Victor was extremely interested in food: buying it, cooking it and eating it. Even as a young boy he apparently spent hours in the kitchen of the family home in St Petersburg, and his specialities were those he learnt in those days. He was a creative, instinctive cook, not weighing things carefully but tossing in this or that and tasting it at every point. He was also a master cook who needed staff, and my role was that of assistant, kitchen-maid and washer-up. I chopped things, under supervision, and washed up the pile of pans and implements he used. He was very knowledgeable about wine; loved choosing it and then serving it to appreciative guests. When William Cowper wrote 'Variety's the very spice of life', he gave Victor a motto. He loved change, and sampling anything new, whether in work, travel, dress or food.

Victor's work as an engineer was as mysterious to me as mine, editing a fashion magazine, was to him; and our respective colleagues were, to each of us, creatures from a different world. I never admired Victor more than during our first months together. He was used to managing a flourishing business; to having a large salary; to running a Bentley. Now he had no car at all; he made difficult journeys by underground and train to visit potential customers, and the workshop in which he was creating the basis of his new business was over a garage in the East End. One Sunday morning he asked me to go with him to this workshop; his colleagues had been at it all night and thought they would have something interesting to show him. All I could see were some bits and pieces of metal, handed around by three exhausted men in need of sleep and a bath. Victor said he thought it was coming along all right. 'It' was the special type of fan on which his budding firm, Plannair, was to be based: extremely small and light, yet producing a powerful stream of air. This was exactly what all aeroplanes needed to cool the various hot spots in their systems; and, before long, Victor was able to tell me that a very large number of the world's airlines used his fans. He was not himself an inventor, but he knew a good inventor when he saw one, and he knew how to finance and manage production and sell the product. Everyone has their skills and their limitations. His inventor colleague possessed none of his skills, and when Victor retired in 1960 Plannair was soon taken over by a large engineering business, which dropped it altogether a few years later.

Looking over farms on behalf of a cousin, we passed the gate of Radley Green Farm, not far from Chelmsford, saw it was for sale and bought it for ourselves. Victor had had a small farm as a sideline during the war, and had loved it. We would be retiring in a few years and would need an interest and a source of income. We scrapped our plans for a holiday in Sardinia and settled in. I was amazed at his energy and organizing ability. Truckloads of every conceivable thing needed on a farm rolled into the yard unceasingly.

Even in the mid-fifties I was struck by the changes that had taken place in the countryside since I was a child. We used to watch tadpoles turn into frogs, and clouds of butterflies sucked nectar from the flowers. Now there were no tadpoles, frogs or butterflies, and wild flowers were almost non-existent. Where there had been fields of cowslips from which we made cowslip balls to hang in the house each spring, people were driving from neighbouring villages to see a few cowslips in our lane. And there were no poppies in our corn.

The farm house itself was a seventeenth-century brick and timber building. There were two large kidney-shaped pools at the back, in one of which we bathed, while the other provided the endless entertainment of carp and goldfish which swam among the water-lilies. We had the best Essex farmland, on which we grew wheat, potatoes and sugar-beet, with enough pasture for our Ayrshire dairy herd. We also kept large white pigs. People expect changes in fashion and furnishing to suit changing tastes, but farm products are subject to the same pressures. The British had become a nation of Jack Spratts, with fewer and fewer who took after his wife. As farmers, our success depended on the diet of our pigs being as carefully weighed as that of a woman entering a weight-losing contest. Farm policy is also influenced by politics. The UK guaranteed a market for Danish bacon; so British pig production was controlled by lowering the market price when a certain level of numbers was reached. Two or three pigs can be kept in a backyard, and that type of pig-keeping can be stopped and started when prices change, but when you have an expensive set-up you have to stick with it.

My tentative suggestion of beekeeping (I love honey) was dismissed by a cautionary tale. 'Where the bee sucks' is at the nearest possible place to the hive; bees are not fussy about their food; all they seek is pollen. Victor knew a man who had lived for the day when he would eat the first honey from his hive – and it was also the last, for the bees had been sucking on a convenient field of onions.

Predecessors at the farm had built on a large kitchen, where we mostly ate. I doubt whether the Aga's simmering oven (with the door open) had ever before housed seven shivering piglets, newborn to a sow that had rejected them. They were given to me to mother, and I marked them A to G in blue chalk so I could be sure that each got its ration of milk from a bottle, three times a day. After a few days of this Victor refused to eat with me, saying that I smelt like a sow. Sadly they died, one by one, beginning with the runt G. Apparently a sow's milk contains some element without which the piglets cannot survive. When the Aga simmering oven contained neither piglets nor the half-drowned hedgehogs we rescued from the ponds, it made wonderful stews, which one left in all night.

To my surprise a vast packing-case turned up at the farm one day. Victor explained that he had always wanted a set of stainless steel cooking pans, so he had ordered some from the Swedish firm who had newly equipped our dairy. There were about two dozen pans in three sizes and, to his great disappointment, I insisted on half of them being sent back. An excellent cook, he used them to great advantage – most famously when Elizabeth David and Anthony Denney came down to the farm for lunch. He was working for *Vogue* as a photographer, and she was contributing her remarkable articles. Victor had prepared for the occasion a unique version of his speciality, borsch. It was just after Christmas and, instead of the usual meat, he had thrown in the considerable remains of our turkey. Elizabeth savoured every mouthful and then gave him the accolade: 'Every now and again, eating a dish, one knows that it is the best of its kind that one will ever eat, and that is how I feel about Victor's borsch.'

But all was not fun on the farm. One Sunday morning, in a winding lane so narrow that cars could only pass by travelling with care, a car rocketed round a bend and drove straight into us. Victor couldn't swerve to the side because there was a deep ditch. This was before the days of seat-belts, and the steering-wheel was driven into his chest, breaking his ribs and his breastbone. His upper lip was nearly sliced off by flying glass. I, in the passenger seat, suffered only cuts and shock. Victor's injuries were agonizing. Even a bruised rib is painful. His were not only broken, but the hospital did not dare to strap them up because the lungs were swollen and needed space to expand. The accident went very close to killing him.

A less serious disaster occurred one bitter winter, when a severe frost formed ice on the ponds so thick that Victor could leap down on it in his heavy farm boots. That was good fun, but we were ignorant of the danger to the fish, which ought to have had a hole in the ice kept open for them to breathe. When the thaw came, only a few had survived, and Victor had the gloomy task of shovelling piles of once-beautiful carp into a wheelbarrow to be dumped and burnt.

For two years we went down to the farm every night. Victor's factory was in Leatherhead, which meant driving through London, morning and evening. He used to drop me on the Embankment, to take the Tube to my office, and he would pick me up there, after work. At the farm we had our meal to get, our mail to look at, and long discussions with our farm manager. For our last three working years we went down only at weekends. And it was at weekends that we fed the pigs, so that our small staff could have a break. We enjoyed it; but it was not the right prescription for my back. And now I suppose I have to say something about the spine trouble that had such an influence on our lives and nearly wrecked our happiness.

In and after the war I had had some slight symptoms, but within a few days of going to live with Victor I had a massive attack that disabled me for weeks. I think it was caused by a combination of physical effort and emotional stress; but it was a bad beginning. In those days even less was known about back trouble than is known today. I went to specialists of all kinds. Victor insisted on my 'taking a cure' at Baden-Baden. He could not leave his fledgling business, so I went alone. It was only seven years after the end of the war, yet Germans actually complained to me about the behaviour of the French, in whose zone they lived: complaints that the French had taken over houses for their officials to live in. When I thought of what the Germans had done in the countries they had occupied I felt outraged astonishment that they should expect my sympathy. On off-days from the cure I went to visit Munich and Nuremberg, amid cries that they had been bombed – 'If only you had seen them before the war!' I felt driven to remark that some English towns had been bombed too, which didn't go down well.

Later, I began to have severe attacks, three or four a year. Sometimes I couldn't move for days on end, and had to lie on the floor of the room where the attack started. I had a sofa at the office and lay down whenever I could. Things were getting impossible. We heard of a Spanish surgeon for whom Lord Nuffield had built an orthopaedic hospital outside Oxford. He was reputed to do miracles with backs by taking a piece of bone from the shin and grafting it on to the spine. I had this rather horrific operation just as I was retiring from Condé Nast. The surgeon assured me that within a few weeks I 'should be able to do anything that a woman of your age could expect to do'. As I was fifty-five, and had good health in every other respect, I expected to do a lot. But it was not to be.

A few months later, when Victor and I were in Moscow for a British Trade Fair – he representing an engineering firm, and I the Wool Marketing Board – I had another attack. An ambulance carried me off to a polyclinic where a surgeon gave me my first blockade (a Russian speciality of pain-killing injections in the nerves leading to the spine). The clinic was staffed with interpreters in all the main languages, which I found very impressive. As I was getting dressed the interpreter said solemnly, 'The surgeon does not like your trousers.' 'Really,' I said. 'What doesn't she like about them?' (Many doctors were women, and, as I was wearing a skirt, she was referring to my underpants.) 'They are not of sufficient thickness.'

That was just the beginning. My spine was always in trouble. I went back to the surgeon three times. He took X-rays, said the operation had been a perfect success and, in the end, washed his hands of me. Some years later a doctor friend said I should go to the top orthopaedic man at Guy's, who had his private practice in the same Harley Street building. After a rather perfunctory examination this specialist said that my problem was nervous, rather than physical, and sent me to the psychiatric ward of Guy's.

This was a strange experience, but, like so many that one

would not have chosen, I came to feel glad that I had had it. There were about twenty of us in this section. One case was very serious. She was a handsome young woman, the daughter of a well-known man, who had made a second marriage when she was a child. She had been sent to boarding-school at an early age and almost totally neglected in the holidays. One Christmas she came home to find the house shut and no message for her. The result, not unnaturally, had been a nervous breakdown on a scale that appeared to be irreversible. When chatting to us, she could be bright and entertaining; but she had violent seizures and, while I was there, reduced her room to havoc by smashing everything in sight. The clinic could not cope and she was sent to an asylum. Whenever I saw her father's name in the papers I wondered what he must feel.

A patient in the cubicle next to me was also young and attractive, half-way through a medical course. She had been in India, where she met an Indian with whom she had fallen in love. She was already engaged to an Englishman, and wanted to make a career in medicine, so she returned to England, whereupon she had a nervous breakdown. We had long talks and I liked her very much; but her fiancé, who visited her, was the original male chauvinist pig: a hearty chap, who used to shout at her, 'Pull yourself together, old girl!' or, 'Come on, old girl, buck up!' I could have murdered him, and obviously it was an impossible relationship that was bound to end in disaster.

During my first days in the clinic I felt able to move easily and was free from pain, so I told my psychiatrist that I had better go home. He said, 'Wait a bit. This is what we call "the period of impossible hope".' And sure enough, I was soon seized by such a stiffness that I could hardly move. Then they began to teach me to relax. I had brought some knitting, remembering that Shurotchka, the wife of Victor's brother in Leningrad, whom I loved and admired, had said that it calmed her when she felt tried beyond endurance. I would sit by the hour and knit, and say over and over again an abracadabra they taught me.

I was the only patient who was given no drugs, and therefore the only one who was allowed – indeed, ordered – to go out alone. At first I could not go more than a few hundred yards to

Audrey Withers at her desk shortly before leaving *Vogue* in 1960
(*photograph by Snowdon*)

Mary Withers, the author's mother, in the garden of Souldern Court in the early 1930s

Monica Withers, the author's sister

Percy Withers, the author's father, in the garden of Souldern Court in the early 1930s

Victor Kennett, the author's husband. This is the best photograph ever taken of him and dates from 1965.

Victor and Audrey Kennett on their Essex farm in the late 1950s

(*above*)
Robert Bridges, the Poet
Laureate, in the garden at
Souldern Court in the late 1920s
(*left*)
A.E. Housman, author of *A
Shropshire Lad*, on a visit to
Souldern Court in the late 1920s

Walnut tree in the garden of Souldern Court
(*watercolour drawing by Paul Nash, 1923*)

Portrait of Percy Withers
(*drawing by William Rothenstein, 1916*)

Caricature of Percy Withers
(*Max Beerbohm, 1916*)

William Rothenstein and
Max Beerbohm (*pencil
drawing by William
Rothenstein; the inscription at
bottom right reads 'Max on his
(almost) native heath. Autumn
at Oakridge Will Rothenstein
Oct 1916'*)

Audrey Withers, aged 19
(*drawing by Paul Nash, 1924*)

be sure of getting back safely. But I walked further and further and reached Southwark Cathedral, where I would sit and rest; and I explored the bank of the Thames where the Globe Theatre has been discovered.

I should explain how I came to land up in a psychiatric ward, for I believe that those who know me would not think me a likely patient. After a major spine operation, the old-style attacks recurred. The surgeon made it clear that I was a nuisance and he didn't want to hear from me again. I was never free from pain and was incapable of doing anything strenuous – a ridiculous situation on a farm, where there are jobs to be done every moment of the day. It was very depressing for Victor as well as for me. He was angry that fate had dealt this blow, and his anger spilled over on to me. Friends told him that he had to accept the fact that his wife was an invalid. A doctor who saw himself as a psychologist said that it could all be put down to my regret at giving up my job. When my medical record was sent, by mistake, to me, I had the pleasure of reading: 'Mrs Kennett is a lady who appears to enjoy ill-health.' My sister Monica gave me a summer-house, so that I could see the countryside when lying down during much of the day. She and Victor had given me up as a permanent neurotic case. I knew that something was physically wrong, but no one would listen. When I had a bad attack in Paris and needed a wheelchair at the airports, I went to the orthopaedic specialist, thinking that he would believe that my trouble was physical; but he sent me back to the psychiatric clinic. To be disbelieved by those nearest to you, as well as by medical advisers, is a devastating experience. You feel isolated, abandoned, and lose all hope. I couldn't believe that neither Victor nor Monica was prepared to fight for me; and so a state of tension set in and I truly did need psychiatric help – for which I was always grateful.

Eight years after my spine operation a new doctor sent me to a surgeon at the London Hospital, who – though X-rays showed nothing amiss – said he would like to 'explore' my spine. Afterwards he said that he had expected to remove a disc, but instead had needed to free a nerve trapped by bone which had grown from the graft. He also screwed some vertebrae together. Naturally it took a while to get over this second operation, but the emotional relief at having my conviction vindicated was as great as the relief from pain. I told my psychiatrist my operation result, and added that among the patients in the ward during my stay, two other women – found to have serious conditions needing surgery – had, like me, been prescribed psychiatric treatment. I begged him to give serious consideration to the possibility of physical conditions in patients referred to him, and he replied that I had given him 'food for thought'.

Of course Victor and Monica were happy at this outcome. Yet neither expressed regret at their disbelief – and I knew better than to make any reference to it. For the most valuable knowledge I gained from my psychiatrist was that there are two types of emotion – one constructive and the other destructive. Of the constructive emotions the greatest is love – as St Paul told us centuries ago; but also such things as kindness, generosity, sympathy, compassion. They are constructive because the giver and the receiver are both enhanced by them. Destructive emotions are anger, hatred, envy, jealousy, guilt, remorse, which can literally destroy all concerned. Deadliest of all is remorse, because it contains no hope of reparation or forgiveness. Guilt is a powerful destroyer of people and relationships, and I was on my guard not to let it injure the two people closest to me.

Farm life had been getting too much for us both. Victor could no longer walk the fields and do farming chores; I was in no condition for much activity; so in 1965 we prepared to sell the farm and move back to London. While Victor coped with the sale I went to London to look for somewhere to live, finally arriving at an attractive little house in Gloucester Place Mews. Victor and I fell for it, and bought it from the proceeds of the farm sale. The only people who never liked it were Victor's family. Misha insisted – from the experience of the River Neva in Leningrad – that we were in danger of being flooded by the Thames. It was useless telling him that we were at least two miles from the river, uphill all the way. His sisters thought it unhealthy to sleep 'below ground'. The bedrooms were a few steps down from the entrance hall, but they were level with a yard at the back, so they were not in a basement. I loved it; indeed it was the favourite of all my London homes. A house has a quality that a flat can never possess. It is an entity in itself, and that entity is yours.

When we moved into Gloucester Place Mews Victor had twelve clocks and I had sixty pictures. I know the number because there were no picture-rails, so he had to hang every one separately, and he counted them. He couldn't be sure of concealing the cord so decided it had better be invisible: and this led him to think of fishing twine, which even an alert fish can't detect. So – always going for the best – he took me off to the most prestigious anglers' paradise, in Pall Mall. A very grand salesman greeted us. 'Fishing twine? Yes, of course, sir. Were you thinking of salmon or trout?' 'I was thinking of hanging pictures,' said Victor, quite unabashed, and as if that was the most obvious thing to do with it. Indeed, I never saw him in the slightest degree put out or embarrassed.

From my father's collection I had inherited a large number of Japanese prints, an Orpen portrait, a Frances Hodgkins still life, landscapes by J.D. Innes, Derwent Lees and John Nash, a Cruikshank, a Griggs etching, Gordon Craig woodcuts and a fine Rossetti drawing of the head of a woman – said to be Adam's mythical first wife, Lilith. Also three Paul Nash watercolours, made during his visits to our Oxfordshire home, and the drawing of me, mentioned earlier. I myself had bought a number of drawings, by Gwen John, David Jones, Ceri Richards, Graham Sutherland, Henry Moore, Barbara Hepworth, Segonzac, two Rouault aquatints, large Villon lithographs of Matisse and Picasso – signed by the artists – and a Vuillard lithograph. My two most spectacular purchases were mine no more. At a summer show of the Redfern Gallery my eye had been caught by a small drawing of a town square. It was an early Picasso, 1898. I bought it for £60, and sold it for a few hundreds when we needed money for the farm. Also at the Redfern I bought (for much the same sum) a large Renoir lithograph of his well-known subject – *Le chapeau epinglé*: the heads of two little girls in big hats. It was an exceptionally fine print, signed, and with chalk marks thought to be Renoir's own. I gave it to Jock for his birthday so, when we separated, he naturally kept it. Later he sold it for £4,000. I did not grudge him the money; but it was the most beautiful thing I have ever possessed, and the only one that I parted from with pain.

We spent ten happy years in Gloucester Place Mews. It was there that Victor began his career as a photographer, aged seventy – ending it when we left. On all our travels he took photographs and developed and printed the black-and-white ones himself. I would record, file and caption everything. After each journey I wrote to all the magazine and book publishers that might be interested, and their picture researchers would come to look at the work and make their choice.

But of course Victor's greatest photographic achievement was the detailed coverage of St Petersburg's finest buildings – which formed the book described later. These pictures were taken in a period when foreign photographers were not allowed such facilities. (We ourselves had been refused official permission.) It was also a period when Russian photographers had great difficulty in getting colour film; and publishing was restricted by a shortage of paper. Restoration of the war damage had begun the moment hostilities ended, so, when Victor set up his camera twenty years later, most of the fabulous interiors had been lovingly re-created. These considerations made me feel that his photographs were of historic interest; and, to safeguard them, I offered them to the Picture Library of the Victoria & Albert Museum, which now holds them.

All good things come to an end. For us, the end came when Victor developed angina pectoris: the same disease which had caused his father to leave Russia in 1918, seeking medical help in Switzerland – and this in turn had brought about Victor's escape, to be with him before he died. Victor's doctor said he must not climb stairs, yet there was no single floor in our little mews house on which one could eat, sleep and wash. So we found a ground-floor flat – and, as it had no space for the photograph collection, and the cameras were too heavy for him to make additions to it, we put it in the hands of an agent, who still finds buyers for it.

6

When Victor and I were first together in 1951 he had had no communication whatever with his Russian family since soon after the war ended in 1945. His mother and sisters were living in Paris. Of course Victor visited them as soon as it was possible, and they began sending letters and an occasional parcel to the family in Leningrad. But, very quickly, they were asked to stop writing. In Stalin's time it could be dangerous even to possess relatives abroad, let alone be in touch with them.

In 1956 an acquaintance of ours rang me up at the office. She was interpreting for the first group of Russian tourists ever to come to England. She asked Victor and me to come and meet them at their Bloomsbury hotel. There were nearly thirty of them, and they immediately formed two groups – one, Russian-speaking, round Victor, and the other, English-speaking, round me. A barrage of questions were fired at us, and no one noticed the time. Suddenly the leader of the party gave a cry: 'We are late again! We were told to have dinner at seven o'clock, and it's half-past.' She asked us to dine with them, and we trooped down sheepishly to a basement dining-room. As we were looking at the menu a virago of a head-waitress came up and cried, 'So you think you can have what you like when you turn up late. Ham for you!' Victor and I were crimson with embarrassment, but one of the group said gently, 'It doesn't matter. We didn't come to England for the food. We have plenty of food at home.'

These were the first native Russians Victor had met since his escape in 1918/19, and naturally he was completely carried away.

He invited a party of about fifteen to come down to the farm for the day. We cooked an enormous Russian meal for them; vodka was tossed off; and then took our visitors to see the farm. We had built a bungalow for our manager and his wife (one of our guests remarked, 'In our country, an admiral would not live like this'). She was quite an accomplished pianist and, open on the piano stand, there happened to be a Tchaikovsky sonata, which impressed our guests enormously. We are all apt to make judgements from a single experience, especially abroad, and I was sure that the Russians would tell friends at home that, in England, all farmers' wives played Tchaikovsky.

Then Victor hired the upper floor of his club to give a dinner party for the whole group. Our only English guests were Marghanita Laski and her husband John Howard. I bought small presents for everyone and put them on their plates, wrapped up like Christmas presents. After dinner there were speeches and toasts till the small hours. On our first visit to Leningrad two years later we were entertained in return, at the House of Architects: an amazing lunch, with three glasses beside each place – for vodka, white and red wine – and waitresses with starched caps and frilly aprons, such as had not been seen in England since the First World War.

During the group's visit Victor had become especially friendly with Leonid Makarieff – formerly an actor, then an actor-manager. Victor told Leonid that he had a brother in Leningrad with whom he had had no contact for years; he didn't even know if he was alive. Would he make inquiries? Months later I was alone at the farm one weekend when a foreign voice on the telephone asked to speak to Victor, saying, 'I have a letter from his brother.' We had had no communication with the USSR but kept in regular touch with Victor's family in Paris, so I assumed that this caller had a letter from his brother-in-law. I asked him to post it, but he was determined to deliver it by hand.

He did. He was an official at the Soviet Embassy, and he brought a letter from Victor's brother Misha. It was in a plain white envelope with only Victor's name on it. When we visited Leningrad the following year and were in Misha's apartment with friends – including Leonid Makarieff – Victor said, 'By the way, Misha, I didn't know that you knew anyone at the Soviet Embassy in London.' 'I don't,' said Misha. 'Well, your first letter was brought by an Embassy official, in an envelope with no address or stamp.' Misha said, 'I addressed the envelope myself, and registered it at the post office.' Victor saw the expression on Leonid's face, and was sure Leonid knew that Misha's letter had been taken out of the post and sent to the Embassy, with instructions that Victor should be reported on. Of course that first group of tourists were all Party members.

Victor had good relations with the Soviet Embassy for several years; but though the contacts were, in his eyes, purely social, some members of its staff hoped to engage his interest in other matters. They knew that, in the course of his business, he visited the engineering works of other firms and thought this gave excellent opportunities for industrial espionage. One official was particularly pressing and wouldn't take his refusals as final. He kept offering him 'a really good car' as a bribe. So Victor invited him to the farm for lunch one weekend and left in the open our rather handsome Rover. His guest noticed it, ate his lunch and departed.

After that meeting with the party of Russian tourists, and the letter delivered through the Soviet Embassy, Victor felt, for the first time, that it would be safe for him to visit the USSR, and we began to make plans. He often said that he couldn't get used to living in a country as small as England. I tried to counter this by saying 'How does it seem so small? There is nowhere you can stand and look over the edge on both sides!' But I made up my mind that, when we went to the Soviet Union, we were going to travel by train every inch of the way, so that I could feel its size for myself. Helsinki was to be our jumping-off place.

The obsession with security, which the Russians have always had, caused them to set up a railway system with tracks of a different width from those in the rest of Europe, so that no train could cross the borders without long delay. Sure enough, at the Finnish-Soviet border the train was emptied and, as it was around dinner-time, we all trooped into an enormous restaurant and ate an enormous meal, while the wheels of the carriages were extended to fit the Russian gauge. The train steamed into

Leningrad well after midnight; and there, on the platform, were five members of the family – of whom Victor knew only one, his brother Misha. The rest were Misha's wonderful wife, Shura; their daughter Yelena and her husband Igor Komarov, a distinguished pianist; and Misha 2, son of Victor's sister, Zina. They were all carrying bunches of flowers. Whatever the difficulty and expense, it is impossible for any Russian to meet a visitor without presenting a bouquet. It has a mystical significance, as I realized when we went to Leningrad the year after Misha and Shura had been allowed to visit us. In a vase in their flat was the bunch of roses I had given to Shura when they left us, shrivelled and brown, but not to be thrown away. So, that first night, we were taken in triumph from the railway station to Misha's flat, where we talked non-stop till dawn.

The family we had met, and to whom we should be closely bound for the rest of our lives, had remarkably interesting talents and careers. None were Party members; indeed I think they took little interest in politics, but kept their heads down and got on with their work – as was necessary for survival during the Reign of Terror of the thirties. Misha was a leading member of a group of architects engaged in rebuilding, conserving and refurnishing the historic buildings that had been damaged in the war. His wife Shura was a distinguished pharmacologist. During the war, she was a colonel in the army medical corps. Misha would joke that he had to salute her when they met, as he was only a captain. Well over military age, he had shown typical courage in volunteering for active service. In fact, he might otherwise have shared the fate of their eldest brother, Leonid, who – together with a million of their fellow-citizens – had died of starvation in the siege of Leningrad. He had been Victor's special friend and companion, and his absence was the only cloud over that homecoming.

Misha had an encyclopedic knowledge of the former St Petersburg's history and its architecture, and so made an incomparable guide, to whom we often introduced people who were visiting the city for the first time. But similar enthusiasm and stamina were required of the guided – as Dickie Buckle, the balletomane, discovered. Misha was asked to take him to the tomb of

Tchaikovsky in Aleksandr Nevsky Lavra and, when they reached it, he fell on his knees in homage. He then expected to return to his hotel, but Misha had other ideas. The Lavra is the graveyard of many of the great names in Russian cultural history, and homage had to be paid to them all. When Nikolaus Pevsner finished his great work on the architecture of the English counties, his grateful publishers offered him a trip to anywhere he liked. He chose Leningrad, and was advised to contact us. We treated him to a private view of Victor's slides, and gave him an introduction to Misha. I think, in that case, enthusiasm and stamina were evenly matched.

It was not till our next visit that we met Victor's sister Zina. She had married a writer, who was executed during the Stalin terror years, and later – an almost more appalling communist practice – rehabilitated. Like her sister-in-law, she had made a distinguished medical career, as a surgeon and as the head of a large hospital in Central Russia. It was in forest country, where there were bears. One winter day a woodcutter, skiing through the snow, caught the tip of his ski above the lair of a hibernating bear. She rushed out at him; he attacked her with his axe; they both fell unconscious in the snow – and were found by another woodcutter, who finished off the bear and got the man to Zina's hospital, where she dealt with his terrible wounds. He was recovering when someone read him a newspaper report that the man who had saved him had been awarded the bounty paid for killing a bear – their numbers were becoming dangerous. 'But that was my bear!' he cried furiously. 'She nearly killed me and I nearly killed her. It's my bounty!' Zina supported him, and he got the bounty.

During those wonderful first days in Leningrad even I could talk, because Misha and Shura both spoke French rather better than I did. It would seem that European countries with difficult languages produce citizens with a special linguistic gift. Also I believe that continental language-teaching is far better than ours; and this is certainly true of Russia. It is ironic that, during a period when Soviet citizens were unlikely ever to meet a national of the country whose language they were learning, let alone to visit that country, they had a far greater mastery of its language than their British counterparts, who were free to travel.

I am ashamed of being unable to speak Russian, but I try to excuse myself by a lot of weighty arguments. When Victor and I came together he did not imagine that he would ever set foot in the USSR again. He deliberately avoided White Russian society. I was still with *Vogue*. When we bought Radley Green Farm in Essex we travelled up and down every day, leaving the farm around 8 a.m. and returning twelve hours later. Then, when we began to visit Leningrad, I found plenty of French and English-speaking people; and the Russian conversations went at an incredible speed, with everyone interrupting and jumping in, so that only an extremely fluent Russian speaker could have taken part in them. I believe if I had been alone, lodging with a Russian family who spoke no other language, I might have managed eventually to stumble along in talk about everyday things.

I took whole courses of Russian lessons: from the farm, driving to a college at Thurrock, and in London at Birkbeck College. There was a happy period when Nicole Marchand, from Paris, was living with us. She had been taking Russian lessons from Victor's sister Lorka, and she came to Birkbeck too. Victor used to coach us, and complained bitterly that one of us had a Ukrainian and the other an Armenian accent, while we were only too pleased that our accents fell within the borders of the USSR at all. We told Victor that if he thought our accents bad, he ought to hear those of our fellow-pupils. One day he did. It was a foggy winter evening, and he offered to drive us to our class. When he went up and introduced himself to our tutor she nearly fell on his neck. 'It's so wonderful to hear Russian spoken correctly!' the poor woman cried. And when the class began to read out loud in turn, Victor could hardly believe his ears. Of course the rest of the students heard Russian only in class, while Nicole and I got it at home also.

As I said earlier, I insisted that, on our first visit to the USSR, the journey there and back should be made by train, so that I could get the feel of the country's size. For many years there were no direct flights between London and Leningrad so, if we were travelling by air, we always had to take a plane or train between Leningrad and Moscow. At the end of that first visit we took a night train. The entire coach was filled with a group of Indian tourists. We got talking, and Victor told them that his son was working in India, at Coimbatore. One man said that he lived not far away, and asked, 'Does your son write to you as often as you would wish?' Victor doubted it. 'When I get home I will visit your son and tell him he should write oftener to his father.' So began a friendship which led to our visits to India some twelve years later.

From Moscow we boarded a train to the Hook of Holland. I certainly felt the size of the country, which was absolutely without landmarks and went on for ever. Poland was, geographically, a continuation of Russia, with only the occasional mound of a stork's nest to break the flatness. We passed through East Germany, West Germany and Holland. I was satisfied, and had no desire to make that journey again.

In all, we must have made ten journeys to the Soviet Union, and one thing that surprised me was that, whether we arrived or left by train, plane or ship, at any hour of the day, at least six relatives and friends would be lined up to greet us or see us off. How did they get away from work? Misha would tell his organization that he wouldn't be in for the next two weeks as his brother from London was visiting him, and it didn't occur to him or anyone else that that absence would be considered as part of his annual leave. I came to realize that the Soviet refusal to allow unemployment, and the insistence that women should work till the age of fifty-five, meant that every organization in the country was overstaffed. People could wander off during working hours to do anything they pleased: join shopping queues, have their hair done, even go to the cinema. They would not be missed, because there was someone else to do the job. Even then women spent an hour or two each day in queues, and, although shops stayed open late (as they didn't, yet, in England), it would have been impossible to deal with everybody if shopping had been left till after working hours.

Several times our journeys to Leningrad were made by little passenger steamers that went from Tilbury up the Baltic. They would stop for several hours at Copenhagen, Stockholm and Helsinki and, as they docked close to the heart of these cities, we had time to explore them. We soon learnt to bring enough of each currency to be able to take a taxi, pay an entrance fee, buy a cup of coffee. We also got to know some of the crew members, who would make clandestine visits to us while their ship was docked at Tilbury, and ask help in finding goods unobtainable at home. Our Russian visitors also enjoyed travelling by these boats, but they suffered the same fate as the transtlantic liners and were discontinued.

The most interesting of our journeys were made by car. We would load the car at Tilbury on a ship bound for Gothenburg. Next day we enjoyed a splendid Swedish lunch: a huge table spread with smorgasbord of every conceivable kind, hot and cold, and a fat, drum-shaped cabinet holding all manner of liquor. Early the next morning the boat docked and we drove with all speed to Stockholm, to catch the night ferry across the Baltic to Turku. From there we crossed Finland, to spend the night in a hotel near the Russian border. Next morning we were in Leningrad.

When one was released by Customs, on the Soviet border, there was a strange drive of several miles through a narrow, high-walled corridor. One could have no idea whether there were actual fortifications there, but it was a security zone. We emerged near the town of Viborg, where we would be met by a nephew, who brought a carful of relatives and friends. We had given cars to three nephews, under a scheme that offered a shopping-list of goods, from cars to boots, to be paid in foreign currency.

Our first journey by car was on our second visit, in 1959, when a foreign make was almost unknown in the USSR. Ours was an open Ford, with a hood that went up and down at the touch of a button. The news spread fast, and each morning, when we came out of the hotel, there was a small crowd standing round the car, waiting to see this magic. One day Victor wanted to shop in Nevsky Prospekt, and left me in the car – which was immediately surrounded by a surging crowd. I could utter only two or three Russian words, and I couldn't understand, let alone answer, the questions that were being hurled at me. So, either in exasperation or for fun, they began to rock the car on its springs, so that I was jumped up and down like a Jack-in-the-box. When Victor returned he had to fight his way through the crowd to rescue me.

Our first visit to Leningrad had been as unreal as a dream. An absence of forty years made the city seem to Victor like a mirage; and to me, of course, everything was strange. Also the visit had been very short, our ambitious plans cut down to size by the stringent currency regulations. But on our second visit the following year, we had clearer heads and more time for sightseeing. I realized that I was looking at wonderful buildings of which the world at large was ignorant, and that Victor and I could make them known through his photographs and my writing. This became possible, eventually, only through the close association of Victor's brother, Misha, with the directors of the museums and palaces of the city. He had merely to murmur a request to his colleagues for us to be able to turn up with full photographic paraphernalia, and spend hours relatively undisturbed, tourism having not yet taken off.

We had permission to use the car within a radius of around 30 kilometres of Leningrad, which was sufficient for us to take in the whole circle of imperial summer palaces. One area in which we photographed was Oranienbaum, which lies beyond Petrodvorets. The architect of the three exquisite buildings was Rinaldi who, as always in the eighteenth century, designed the interiors as well as the exteriors. Victor was busy working in the Chinese Palace when a voice on the loudspeaker demanded that the owner of a certain car should come to the entrance. Of course it was ours, and a KGB colonel told Victor that foreign cars were not allowed in that area. He agreed that we were within the 30 kilometres limit, but said that the area was prohibited on account of the presence of a nuclear laboratory. We were to leave at once. However, Victor argued that the harm, if any, had been done: there we were, and we would not come again. But he needed another two hours to finish his work, so could he please stay? The colonel agreed. Of course it made all the difference that Victor spoke Russian, but over and above that were Victor's remarkable powers of persuasion. He was never either aggressive or wheedling. He simply stated his case with such conviction that there was no choice but to agree. This was the secret of his salesmanship; I have heard him clinch a large deal over the telephone with someone he had not even met.

One is so used, in England, to having a friendly relationship with shop assistants that it was a shock to feel the antagonism between customers and staff in the USSR. But then I remembered the war years, when goods were scarce and one was often met with a curt refusal, and I realized that this situation had persisted throughout the lifetime of everyone concerned. After all, the whole business of buying and selling can go smoothly only if the goods are there; and, when they aren't, both sides feel a frustration that can turn to anger. I sensed another element in this relationship. Communist ideology does not include – indeed positively rejects – any conception of 'service', except to the Party and the State. So I think that people working in service industries resented their position, which made them do as little as possible – and that little, grudgingly.

Nevertheless this attitude could be transformed by a human approach. Victor and I went to a shop selling music records. The only assistant was a young woman who sat at a table, looking bored and totally uninterested in everybody and everything. After a brief look round, Victor decided he needed help and went up to her. She scowled at him, as if daring him to bother her. Then he said, 'Couldn't you smile at me?' At which she was so astonished that she did indeed smile, got to her feet and showed him where to find the records he wanted. He was probably the first person who had ever addressed her as a human being.

He brought off a coup in much more difficult circumstances. We were returning to London carrying two huge jars holding about a kilo of caviare, to which a whole group of friends had contributed; and it was forbidden to take more than a few grams out of the country. Victor tackled an intimidating woman Customs officer who was examining luggage. Our holiday had come to an end, we had had such a wonderful time. Had she had a holiday? In the Crimea? Beautiful; he knew just where she had been. As they chatted, she took a piece of chalk and absent-mindedly marked our suitcases. I have never known anyone (except my father) with such complete social confidence. It never occurred to Victor that anyone could fail to respond – and it worked like a charm, in any language, all over the world. Being with him, I was drawn into the life of every place we visited.

Few visitors from the West could be seen in Russia in those days, so we had curiosity value. But much more. Victor was given a huge welcome, as a Russian of whom they could ask questions about the outside world. I had my uses too. Through those high-powered Soviet tourists we had entertained in England – at least half of whom were English-speaking – we were caught up in a group of academics who taught my language and literature, and relished the chance of conversation. They also got to know that I would send them books. Our lecturer friends knew many of the English classics, but they longed for modern novels, from which they would get a feel of the way the language was used today. So I would get lists of authors and titles from them – and also supplied the needs of artists, architects, actors and historians, adding a liberal sprinkling of Agatha Christie, by request. Some thirty years after our first visit, I thought – before throwing away my card index – that I would tot up the number of books I had sent. There were over six hundred.

We did a feature for *House & Garden* showing the flats of friends – naming them simply by their professions. The father of one had possessed a large collection of paintings, taken over, during the Revolution, by the Russian Museum. Their single room in a communal flat – one shared kitchen and bathroom – contained a few treasures. They gave us an elaborate dinner, ending with tea served in magnificent cups. Our hostess said, 'Yes, they are lovely. The Hermitage have only two cups, but you see we have a whole service.'

We had friends on the staff of the Herzen Institute, which specialized in the teaching of languages. On a visit in 1967 I was invited to give a series of lectures to post-graduate students. I said I did not know enough about their training to lecture, but proposed instead to read them poetry from Elizabethan to modern times – which we could discuss. When we reached T.S. Eliot I chose his poem *The Journey of the Magi*. A member of the Institute staff sat in on every session – silent, but all ears – so I was very careful what I said. In this case I asked whether anyone knew who the Magi were? No. The Three Wise Men? No. So I gave them an outline of the event in which the Magi played their part. When I told them about Herod sending his soldiers to kill the young children, they were horrified. 'To kill children?' they cried. 'That's the story.' I told them that the themes of *The Magi* and *The Massacre of the Innocents* were favourites of painters, of which I felt sure that they would find examples in the Hermitage. When I got back to London I went round the galleries, bought postcards of every example I could find, and sent them off. I had several letters in reply, saying that they had indeed found such paintings in the Hermitage.

It seems to me that whole areas of art and music and literature lose much of their meaning for those who do not know Bible stories. The Hermitage possesses a roomful of Rembrandts, including *The Prodigal Son*, than which I think there is no greater painting. Another is a scene in which David hands to Uriah – whose wife, Bathsheba, he has seduced – a dispatch ordering him to be put in the front of the battle, upon which Uriah senses that he has been handed his death warrant. In the background is the scribe, an onlooker in this drama. To anyone ignorant of the story it would simply be a painting of three men. They could hardly sense the tension, and it wouldn't stay in their memory.

After one of those poetry readings at the Herzen Institute I was seized by a student called Nick. A young American visiting the Institute had said something strange, which they didn't understand: 'Why does an elephant wear tennis shoes?' I told Nick that it sounded like the first part of a riddle. He said, 'Please?' So I described what was meant by a riddle, and explained that the question never made sense until you knew the answer. Couldn't he ask the American? He had gone back to the States. I said I was sorry, I couldn't help. Then, from the depths of my subconscious, something rose to the surface and I said, 'Nick, I believe the answer is "Because he can't pack them in his trunk."' 'Please?' So I explained the two meanings of 'trunk', and he ran off to tell his friends the good news. My stock rose sky-high. The riddle-solving made more impression than hours of poetry reading. And, talking of hours, when finally I collected my earnings from the bursar, I had been coming to the Institute for three hours, twice a week, for six weeks. I was looking forward to leaving a nice little sum with Misha. Little it was, too. My fee was one rouble an hour, which made 36 roubles – at the official exchange, the equivalent of £36, but at the realistic black-market rate, about £7.50.

We were going to Leningrad almost every year, so we made many friends. As we were working during the day we had to refuse lunch invitations, but happily accepted those for late after-noon or evening, though we could never be sure what we should get to eat. When we thought it would be a cup of tea, we might get a three-course meal. On the other hand, when we expected dinner, it might be just coffee and cake. Russians are the most generous of hosts and, knowing the difficulty of providing food, we often begged our friends to give us a simple meal. But such an idea is so alien to a Russian that we were wasting our breath; they always need to provide far more than their guests can eat. Often, long after we had finished, the bell would ring, unex-pected friends would appear and they would be given a full-dress meal. With us, if such a thing happened, we would say we were so sorry, we had finished dinner. What about a drink? And, in England, they would ring up in advance – whereas there, they just ring the bell.

Simply to ring the bell of a Russian home is enough to get the full-dress guest treatment – as Victor relearnt when I was doing my poetry readings at the Herzen Institute. He and Misha were just leaving for a photographic session when a friend of Misha's turned up with photographs to show Victor. He had not told Misha that he meant to come. Victor, the Westerner, said he was very sorry, he would have been most interested, but they had an appointment to keep – could he come back another day? As they got into the car Misha said, 'We have not behaved like true Russians. We ought to have stayed and looked at my friend's photographs.' Victor protested, 'But we had an appointment. It would have been rude not to keep it – and they might have refused to make another.' Misha was adamant and, as a Russian, he was right, for his friend was so offended that he never appeared again.

Our English friends often remarked that it was strange that the Soviet Government should spend vast sums on the restoration of palaces that had been built by rulers and aristocrats wiped out by the Revolution. The answer lay in the need of every nation to possess emblems of its history, and the Russians have a fervent pride in their heritage. Schoolchildren, students, soldiers and sailors were taken around to see the treasures of museums, galleries and even churches such as Petropavlovsky, where the tsars are buried. The people were brought up with a great respect for such things: as appeared from a tale told us by the learned secretary of the Hermitage, which has barriers to prevent the public from getting too near the paintings. If the barrier was breached, an alarm bell rang in her office and she had to check up on it. Usually it was because the crowd had pushed against the rope. So it was decreed that the maximum number of visitors should be 30,000 – the precise number admitted to imperial receptions before the Revolution. One January day this figure was reported and the doors closed, but later it struck the secretary that people might be waiting outside in the bitter cold. She looked out on the Neva embankment, saw a long queue standing in the snow, and told reception to open the doors and give everyone hot drinks. She said that, at New Year, visitors came from all over the USSR and that they wouldn't dream of going home without visiting the Hermitage.

It is very easy to make the mistake of thinking that if a regime is 'wrong' in our eyes, everything it does is wrong: though we know very well that not everything done by an acceptable regime is 'right'. The Soviet Union had a system of child care far more developed than we have ever had in the United Kingdom, even in wartime. I researched into the system in the USSR and Bulgaria for an article which *The Guardian* wanted, and found careful planning in both countries. Everywhere there were kindergartens and crèches where women could leave their children in expert care, from babyhood. The mother's workplace telephone number was noted and, if the child became ill, the mother was called, she would be released from work, and would be expected to stay with her child at home for as long as was necessary. There was no such thing as a latchkey child. In the case of all children not considered old enough to be on the streets alone, they were kept at school, resting, playing or doing homework; and staff stayed on until the last child had been collected.

The fact that all women worked till the age of fifty-five meant that provision had to be made for schoolchildren in the holidays. Children were all 'pioneers', and their group organized activities. The Leningrad headquarters were in the former Anichkov Palace where, as usual, a few rooms were preserved with their original furnishings. The children passed through them, but not one would have dreamt of touching anything. The activities consisted of dancing classes – ballet and modern; classes teaching various foreign languages; and one room was filled with small tables, at each of which sat two children playing chess – with an instructor going the rounds. No wonder Russia has gained so many chess championships. In addition to all this, parties of children were taken on outings of every kind, from museums to swimming-pools.

Another welcome provision was made by the Soviet system for its workers, in the shape of health centres and rest homes. There were facilities in spas; holiday hostels on the Black Sea; and, for those in the professions, specially built complexes in the countryside. We went out to visit friends staying in the Writers' Rest Home at Zelinagorsk. They had a two-room apartment, took their meals in the restaurant, had the use of a large library, and the companionship of colleagues when they wanted it – all at charges much lower than for a hotel. In Leningrad itself each of the professions possessed, as a club, one of the beautiful small palaces formerly belonging to a noble family. Again, a few rooms would be preserved in their original state, and the rest adapted to contemporary purposes.

Litter was simply non-existent. One never saw a scrap of paper or a cigarette-stub on the streets or pavements, which in itself was a powerful element in litter prevention. Public transport was excellent. It had to be, for only a tiny minority had cars. There were buses, trolley-buses and trams, and we rarely waited for more than two or three minutes. The elderly, and those with young children, entered by a door in front and, if all the seats were occupied, younger people immediately got up. When they extended the Metro there was a brilliant innovation. At the foot of the escalator – moving half again as fast as ours – was a wide hall with apparently solid walls on both sides. Would-be passengers stood in groups, and when the train came in, the walls split into opening doors beside these groups. Passengers came out, others went in. There was no pushing and shoving; no one could fall on the track.

At the Mariensky Theatre for opera and ballet we saw an elderly woman walking down the stalls, looking for her seat. She was obviously a peasant, in simple country clothes with a scarf over her head, and she was alone. But she walked with perfect composure, as if it was the most natural thing in the world for her to be there. To us it was such an unusual sight that we commented on it. 'Oh yes,' said our friends. 'She will be a worker on a co-operative farm. They give a prize of some sort – like a theatre ticket – to a worker who has done well, or fulfilled so many years on the farm. It's much appreciated.' It was impossible to imagine this happening at Covent Garden.

Of course, while in Leningrad I was mainly a prop in Victor's performance – and a virtuoso performance it was. Victor spoke fluent English, he had a huge vocabulary and was uninhibited in any language, but when he spoke Russian among Russians he displayed a sort of exuberant ease, as of a fish swimming in home waters. You had only to watch his friends' faces to know that he was eloquent, fascinating and funny. I sat by the hour with a tide of Russian pouring over me – picking up enough to catch the gist of what was being said, and managing to laugh or look serious at the right places. I noticed a Russian habit of speech that was very different from ours. In England we never say a plain 'No'; it is always softened. But during those excited conversations I would often hear 'Nyet' hurled at Victor in a tone that seemed to convey utter contempt but was simply meant to express disagreement. One of those stories that go around in censored countries was of Stalin and Molotov getting a telephone call from an overseas ambassador. Molotov, taking the call, simply said 'Nyet' at intervals – then, finally, 'Da', and put down the receiver. 'Why did you say "Da"?' demanded Stalin. 'Because he asked whether it was snowing here.'

I think politics was rarely discussed. The people we knew were not dissidents. They were academics, artists, architects – a few of whom were Party members. Someone might grumble to Victor, knowing that it would go no further. But I remember one occasion which made me realize how all-pervading was the Party-line control of the arts. We had seen a new ballet and were greatly impressed. The theme was of Prince Igor who, with his whole army, had been captured by the enemy and was finally released to return to his country, almost alone. In the Russian myth he is a great hero, but the ballet theme stepped out of line, showing him as shunned and reviled on his return, with women gesturing – Where is my husband? Where is my son? The next day we went to the home of Leonid Makarieff, the actor-manager from the original tourist group. His wife was an actress; their whole life had been in the theatre; Leonid had worked with Chaliapin and had many mementoes of him. Victor mentioned this ballet – then, before he could enlarge upon it, Leonid burst out angrily that it was outrageous, should never have been allowed, and that they were going to see that it was taken off immediately.

For a time, in the Khrushchev era, it seemed that the cultural grip was loosening. On one visit, excited friends told us that a committee which controlled book publication had thrown off the most hard line of its members. Then there was the first exhibition of modern art in Moscow. Khrushchev detested it and wanted it to be closed, but agreed to attend a meeting of people influential in the arts. One by one they got up and argued the case, saying that the Soviet Union would be a laughing-stock if its people were not even allowed to see paintings that the rest of the world admired. And though he growled, 'Don't expect me to admire them', they won the day. 'He is someone you can argue with,' people said.

Occasionally a Party member would tell Victor an inside story. One concerned the death of Stalin, who was paranoiac about security. He had left the Kremlin for a specially designed dacha, consisting of three identical rooms opening on to a corridor. There was only one other room, for a bodyguard, who was instructed to leave Stalin's meals on a table in the corridor and go away. When the coast was clear, Stalin would come out of whichever room he was occupying and take in the tray. Late one night the bodyguard telephoned in alarm: he had gone out to take away the empty tray, but it had not been touched. The entire Politburo was alerted and a procession of large black Zims drove out through the night. Doors were broken down and Stalin was found unconscious on the floor. Beria, the sinister head of the KGB, cried out, 'The tyrant is dead!' At that moment, Stalin opened one rolling eye. Beria fell on his knees, crying 'My master!' Then the eye shut and the tyrant *was* dead.

The most un-Russian of our circle was Victor's closest friend, Alexander Sergeyevich Titov, to whom – with Misha – we dedicated our book, *The Palaces of Leningrad*. He was un-Russian in his appearance, being over six feet tall, and slender. He had a passion for cars, guns and photography – passions that Victor shared. On the floor of his flat there was the skin of a bear he had shot. He was training a young pointer bitch; and one winter evening, when he was taking us to the Metro station, she came with us. He gave her the order, 'Wait here!'. Whereupon she lay down in the snow while we went on out of sight. Then he whistled, and she galloped up. He was one of the very few people I have known whose optimism never faltered. If one plan was impossible, something else could be done. With him, one felt confident that all would be well. But there was one occasion when Alexander didn't get away with it. He was with us on a photographic session in Oranienbaum. Groups of visitors were disturbing the work, which he remedied by bolting the door to keep them out. Peace prevailed, the work was finished, and we moved on to another of the beautiful small palaces in the group. But our behaviour had been reported, and it was not long before a call came through, 'Throw the rascals out!'

Victor loved to have Alexander with him when he was photographing because he was so tall that he could get shots from a higher tripod. He was the head of a machine-design team working in Engineers Castle, which was top-secret territory, but he smuggled Victor in to take a quick shot of a very striking double-eagle emblem, dating from the time when it was the palace of Paul I. I was told to wait in the street outside; but when they came out he took me by the arm, put his finger to his lips (he spoke only Russian) and led me to the staircase to see the eagle. He was a darling man.

Two years after that momentous first visit to Leningrad, Victor's brother Misha and his wife got permission to visit us. In those intensely Cold War days that was a remarkable tribute to the degree of trust which the Soviet authorities placed in them and us. Misha was a leading figure in Leningrad's restoration programme; his wife was an eminent medical specialist: citizens whom the Soviet Union could not afford to lose. (Of course they had left behind a 'hostage' family in the shape of a daughter, son-in-law and granddaughter.) We drove them in a great loop from Yorkshire to Somerset and Kent, taking in cathedrals, abbeys and historic houses.

In London we had made a special arrangement for Misha (who had worked on the restoration of St Isaac's Cathedral in Leningrad) to be taken over St Paul's by Lord Mottistone, who was in charge of its restoration. Victor went along as the interpreter. The two architects had hardly shaken hands before they disappeared up a ladder that seemed to reach the sky. Victor, not at his happiest with heights, was left on the cathedral floor under the sympathetic grins of the builders, but he quickly followed the two men up, knowing that they could not communicate without him. Lord Mottistone showed them where a single gigantic oak beam had spanned the dome and been splintered by a bomb. Realizing how vulnerable and vital the beam was, they had prepared a steel girder of similar size to take its place. Without it, the dome would have collapsed.

St Paul's was then standing in an immense empty space, from which every other building had been swept away by bombs and fire. When Misha came again, a few year later, that space had been filled by tall office blocks which crowded in on the cathedral. He was outraged, and with reason. It was an occasion when his own authoritarian government would have safeguarded a national symbol better than our democratic one was prepared to do. The architect and town planner, Sir Patrick Abercrombie (brother of my father's friend Lascelles, of whom more later), had been commissioned to draw up a plan for that area, which would have safeguarded the site, but it was shelved. Every foot of the land was owned by some company, which could not be robbed or compensated, and building ambitions went higher than before. So St Paul's lost its skyline pre-eminence and London lost a landmark.

The safe return of those first Russian visitors made possible the later visit of their daughter and her husband, Igor Komarov, a very fine pianist. Daniel Barenboim had organized a summer festival on the South Bank and we took them to hear a fine performance of Schubert's Trout Quintet, with Barenboim and his wife, Jacqueline du Pré, among the players. Igor longed to meet Barenboim and I made the request. But it was the summer of 1968; at that moment Russian tanks rolled into Prague, and Barenboim refused to meet a citizen of the Soviet Union.

In 1965 Misha's wife Shura (whose character was as fine as her looks) died, and he was distraught. We had invited him to visit us, but his travel application had been twice refused. He begged us to meet him in Moscow, where he hoped that Victor could help him to win his case. So we all went to the KGB, where a colonel asked Misha why he was making so much fuss. Why did he want to go to England? He had already been there – once was enough. Victor told the colonel of things we had done for the USSR. We had entertained the cast of a famous Moscow theatrical company when they played in London. I had written, and he had illustrated, a feature on Leningrad, which should encourage tourism. Throughout, Misha displayed admirable dignity; Victor's presence was doubtless a support. The colonel told Misha to write a statement as to why he thought he should visit England and bring it to him next morning, adding, 'And come without your brother.' So Misha did just that. Our hearts sank when he returned; the colonel was not there; his note would simply be binned. But a few days later the visa office reopened his case and he was given permission to stay with us. As a Party member once said to Victor, 'Even we never know whether the answer will be Yes or No.'

That a senior KGB officer could spare time for a lengthy discussion with a retired architect about a visit to his brother is an example of something I found almost as alarming as the more brutal forms of communist power. There was nothing too trivial, in the lives of the most unimportant people, which did not come under scrutiny, and an unlimited number of people were willing to carry out such scrutiny. In fact there was not an organization of any kind – factory, shop, office, college or school – that did not have its quota of KGB informers; and we were very shaken to realize that some of the Russians with whom we had become friendly were of that number.

The authorities were obsessive about anything leaving the country, as we found when we were in Leningrad to celebrate Victor's eightieth birthday. He had gifts from the personal possessions of friends: an engraving, a lithograph, two portions of a tiny icon triptych. One such present had been mentioned on the telephone – which must have been tapped, because when we left, everything was tipped out of our suitcases and every present seized. All the more remarkable, then, was the story of Fabergé's business partner whose sons had been at school with Victor. Emigrating during the Revolution, he planned to get the greatest possible value out of the country by half filling a vacuum flask with gems, then sealing them with wax, topped up with coffee. There was chaos when the train stopped at the border. Revolutionary guards were seizing everything. One pounced upon the flask, and, told it was only coffee, tossed it out of the window. Its owner said calmly, 'Well you've probably broken it, but if you'll kindly hand it back, I could at least strain my coffee from it.' And he did; and the family lived on the contents for years.

The close friendship with several professors and lecturers at the Herzen Institute made us want to give the Institute a present. We decided on the *Oxford English Dictionary*, in all its volumes. They were addressed to the head of the English department, but never arrived: the University had heard they were in a Customs shed and had grabbed them. Quite undeterred, Victor ordered a second set, took it to the Soviet Embassy, and asked them to send it to the proper address in their diplomatic bag. The Institute, in gratitude, gave us and Misha a trip to the island of Kizhi, in Lake Onega, where there is a fascinating spread of early wooden churches and farmhouses, brought piece by piece from distant northern regions and re-erected in a more accessible area. We should never otherwise have seen this beautiful aspect of ancient Russian architecture. The restriction placed on us was that we had to make the journey, each way, by night, as we should be passing through an area barred to foreigners, and might see some unauthorized sight from the train windows.

Our last photographic session in the autumn of 1971 was a bit of a cliff-hanger. We had been in Leningrad for only about two weeks when the Macmillan government expelled 102 'spies' from the Soviet Embassy. Friends called us up anxiously and advised us to get out of the country without delay. Victor was determined to complete his work by photographing the last palace on our list. It had become a home for retired military men. But Misha knew that, as usual, at least two reception-rooms had been preserved in their original state. We drove over one of the Neva bridges and turned into a blind road, occupied by the palace. Another car drew up and an officer shouted, 'You are standing on a military point!' Victor replied that he was intending merely to photograph one or two rooms of the palace. 'You will do nothing of the sort. I advise you to go home, and to take no more photographs.' After that Victor felt it would be unwise to drive about in a car that had GB number-plates and carried photographic equipment. He even decided to have his black-and-white film developed and contact printed, so that the border guards would see that it was harmless. When we loaded up to drive out, Victor put all his photographs in a bag, kept behind my knees, with a rug spread over the top. After all these precautions, an anticlimax: the Customs officers never asked me to get out of the car and did not look for anything.

All our travelling and photography were done on our own initiative, and afterwards we thought how best to use them. One commission came Victor's way: to illustrate a book on Tchaikovsky which John Warrack was writing. Unfortunately this came at the time when I was working to a deadline on the text for our book, so I could not go with him. Victor hated to be alone, and it proved to be an awkward assignment. John Warrack had been in Russia and had naturally visited Tchaikovsky's house, now a museum filled with memorabilia. Naturally, also, he had written to its director, telling her of Victor's prospective arrival and counting on her help. To a Westerner it was an obvious thing to do. But the Russian official mind works in its own way, and it has a great suspicion of anyone but a Russian dealing with a Russian subject. We ourselves, when embarking on our book, had begun with an approach to the Ministry of Culture and had the door slammed in our face. Only Misha's old-boy-network approach had made Victor's photography possible. So when John Warrack's letter arrived, the director asked the Ministry what she should do, and was told to bar the door.

This was a serious blow; there was nothing for Victor to photograph in the Moscow region but the statue of Tchaikovsky, depicted writing a symphony while an angel hovered overhead. As Victor worked, he saw a man watching him, recognized him and realized he was being shadowed. When he had finished, he beckoned to the man and said, 'Would you help me put my things together? Then I'll get a taxi. I think we are going the same way.' The chap meekly obeyed, but, as the taxi slowed to turn in at the hotel entrance, he jumped out and ran away. Victor had better luck in Leningrad, where the Theatre Museum had not heard of the Ministry's veto. They welcomed him enthusiastically, and he and his nephew spent happy hours there. But pictures of the forbidden Tchaikovsky Museum were still needed. A Russian photographer was engaged to take them and Victor had to provide him with colour film.

The passport stage of leaving the USSR was always prolonged and tense. KGB officers would look at the passport photograph, then at your face, then back to the passport and back to your face – until you began to wonder whether you really were the same person. Obviously they would be in serious trouble if someone unauthorized managed to slip out. However, it was only at the end of what was to be our last visit together that we had a really alarming experience. We had taken a six-day tour to Moscow and Leningrad because Victor was too ill for us to make the usual six-month-ahead application for a private visit. We arrived in Leningrad in March, when it was still very cold. The window of our hotel room wouldn't close; he was shivering, and said he was not going to stay there. I went to reception to ask for another room; of course I was told that they were all occupied. He then called up his niece to ask whether we could stay two nights with her, and told reception that we were leaving for her flat. I never questioned anything Victor did in Russia. It was his country, his language, his family. He always did anything he was determined to do; and, since he was ill, it would have been impossible to argue with him. But I thought to myself – how can we go and stay in a private apartment at a moment's notice, when it takes six months to get permission to do so?

We had not been half an hour with our niece when the telephone rang. It was the KGB. The hotel, of course, had alerted them. Victor explained the reasons for his move, and said that we would be back at the hotel for the third night, ready for an early start the next morning. At the airport we checked in and were already in the departure lounge when a voice on the loud-speaker asked for Mr Kennett to return. There was a query about his luggage. As Victor went back through the barrier I saw him being marched off between two KGB officers. It was very fright-ening. With his heart condition, the least disturbance could bring on an attack. It seemed that an age went by before he reappeared, alone, very pale and quiet. He didn't say a word until after the plane took off. The he told me that he had been taken to a room, stripped to his underpants, and the officers had then turned out his pockets and run their hands down the seams of his clothes. They found nothing. He had asked, 'Are you satisfied?' No reply. 'Do you think that a sick old man would be so foolish as to play tricks in your hospitable country?' No reply. They walked out and left him. The whole affair was simply a punishment for breaking the rules.

After this our journeys narrowed down to visiting relatives in Switzerland and France – the last one made after Victor's sister's tragic death, when Victor himself was very near the end of his life. She was killed in the streets of Nice by a boy visitor, who had jumped on his host's motor cycle without finding out how to apply the brakes. Victor was so ill that he needed not only wheelchairs at the airports but lifting tackle to get him into the plane. His devotion to his family made him indomitable.

7

Travel to the Continent with a car, in the fifties, was the easiest, most casual thing imaginable. Some enterprising characters had got together a few old bombers and cleared out their interiors to make room for a couple of cars, plus seats for their passengers and two or three others. On our first holiday together Victor and I drove down to Eastleigh. Ours was the only car booked on that flight to Cherbourg, and after a few minutes we were asked, 'Would you mind waiting a moment? Your pilot is listening to the Test Match in Australia.' When we took off it seemed like another few minutes before we landed on a cliff-top, where there was a small hut, housing a couple of uninterested Customs officers. After handshakings and 'Bons voyages!' we were on the road south. The only time Customs took any interest in us was in Deauville, where we were asked if we were bringing presents. We were taking a clock and several pictures to Victor's sister and her husband for their new flat in Nice. Victor made a characteristic response: 'Presents? I expect to be given presents.' And we were waved through.

After that first flight to Cherbourg we arrived, late and tired, in Bordeaux, and woke to a loud hum of activity. The whole square had become a market, roofed in with striped canvas and lined with stalls. We stopped to gaze at a lump of butter the size of a barrel, presided over by a beaming woman of much the same size. Victor told her that we had not seen so much butter for years; to which she responded by holding out a kilo to us on the point of an enormous knife. We had to explain that we were beginning a holiday and that it would melt in the car. Not that the weather was hot, a consistent feature in all our holidays. It was disappointing for Victor, who loved the heat and would have liked to lie on a beach. However, it suited me, since I regarded a holiday abroad as an opportunity for sightseeing.

After losing our stakes at the Biarritz casino we drove the whole length of the Pyrenees to Perpignan. As we rounded a bend, an eagle rose from its meal at the roadside and almost grazed the bonnet. We saw a whole flight of eagles, which were mounting into the sky on an air current, without moving their wings. From Perpignan we went to two concerts in a series which Pablo Casals gave each summer in the semi-ruined abbey of Prades, where he held a summer school. It was an extraordinary experience, even in the intervals, when we went out into a silence broken only by the call of a night-bird, for the audience stood quietly, speaking in whispers.

We had heard that there was a man who drove a jeep up a mountain track impossible for cars, and that he would take about half a dozen passengers. After climbing around you could have something to eat at a small chalet. It was a hairpin track, skirting the edge of precipices. The chalet, with three or four rickety tables set out in front, stood in an upland meadow between the peaks. Our small group scattered on the mountainsides and we climbed alone, skirting patches brilliantly blue with gentians. Then we came down for lunch, expecting to get cold meat and salad, but found the menu of a very good restaurant. Astonished and intrigued, we went into the chalet to congratulate them, whereupon the mystery was solved. The chef had been with a leading Paris restaurant. He had had a nervous breakdown, could not take the pressures of Paris life but had a passion for cooking, so he and his family spent the summer at the chalet. The jeep brought the provisions; and he enjoyed producing *haute cuisine* in the high Pyrenees.

One year I read an article about the Aeolian Islands, and a new hotel which had been built on Lipari. We planned to drive to Messina, take the ferry to Sicily, and leave the car at the port from which boats went to the islands. The hotel was perfect; extremely simple, but furnished with great taste. The only sinister element was the father of the two young men who ran it. He would stand inside the restaurant door, his dark business suit contrasting with the holiday clothes of the guests, his eyes, behind dark glasses, resting on each table in turn. We felt sure that only a member of the Mafia would have had the privilege of building the first hotel on the island.

We had left our car in Cefalù, from where the boats went to and fro to Lipari. On our return we explored the little town, where the sites for selling the catch are marked out by mosaic pictures of fish, let into the pavements. The superb cathedral was the work of those master builders, the Normans. Not content with crossing the Channel and taking over England, they had braved the Bay of Biscay and sailed the Mediterranean to occupy Sicily. And there also they showed their remarkable gift as colonizers. They built cathedrals, decorated with mosaics depicting Bible stories; and they won the collaboration of the Muslim community, who created mosaic panels of exquisite abstract designs. It is the pairing of these two elements that makes the cathedrals of Sicily unique. Victor lay on his back under the apse of Cefalù Cathedral, pointing his lens at the mosaic, high above, of *Christ in Power*, with four seraphim fluttering in the corners of the dome. Later it was chosen from a great number of other candidates, to make the dust-jacket of Malcolm Muggeridge's book, *Jesus: The Man Who Lives*.

If we suspected the presence of the Mafia on the island of Lipari, there was more about the Mafia during our visit to Sicily itself. Victor always studied bills presented to him and questioned anything he did not understand. Twice – when he had bought shoes and had a haircut – the bill included a percentage added beneath the cost of the item. Each time he asked, 'What is this?' And each time he was answered by a shrug of the shoulders and a muttered, 'Surely you understand.' The percentage was Mafia protection money.

Bandits almost came into our lives. We left our Palermo hotel to drive to Agrigento, Selinunte and Segesta. On our return the staff fell upon us, asking if we were all right. They said that on the day when we were driving by the only road across the island, bandits had descended from the hills and held up the passing traffic. They had gone through every vehicle, stripping passengers of jewellery, watches and money. A coach passenger reported that one man had sat quietly amid the uproar. When the bandits reached him he simply said, 'Don't touch me', and they didn't. He was a member of the Mafia.

We turned up one day at Piazza Armerina, where the Roman emperors had had a hunting-lodge. The tessellated pavements showed hunting scenes with wild boar, deer and even ostriches, but the floors were so dusty that the mosaics were dull and blurred. While we were brooding on this problem an obviously professional group arrived, and the custodian asked us to stand aside because they were to take photographs for a German magazine. Then to our delight the camera crew asked for the floors to be washed. A hose was turned on, the colours sprang to life, and we discreetly followed on the heels of the crew, to catch our subjects while they were still glistening brightly.

But if we had good luck with mosaics, we were to have our usual bad luck with the weather. Victor jibbed at the prospect of driving all the way back from the toe of Italy, and we cut the journey by taking a car ferry to Naples. It was a night crossing, and I imagined waking up to a wonderful view of the bay. I should have known better. The fog was so thick that we never saw land until we bumped against the quay. We crawled out of Naples to Pompeii, of which we could just distinguish one building at a time. Vesuvius might not have existed.

There was no point in stopping around; the fog could be shaken off only by driving north, and we had done so before reaching Tarquinia and its wonderful relics of the Etruscan age. From a graveyard on the hillside several tomb-chambers had been excavated and brought to rest in the museum established in a fine Renaissance *palazzo*. The walls of each chamber were covered with frescoes illustrating the life of its occupant: sport and hunting for one young man; banquets and family life for an older one. Funeral statues were displayed in the great hall. On each high pedestal was a reclining figure – not lying flat, as in our medieval tombs, but raised by a cushion or propped on an elbow, lifelike, as guests at a banquet. These portrait sculptures had features of great distinction and perfect serenity. The Etruscans

136

are a mysterious people of whom little is known; but they must have possessed a faith which gave them confidence that death was not to be feared.

Victor shared the continental belief in spas, and, when my back and his shoulder were giving trouble, we decided to go to Bad Gastein. We drove across a stretch of Germany, and when darkness began to fall while we were on the autobahn, Victor decided to turn off, saying that there would be an inn in every village. Soon there was indeed an inn, and he rang the bell at a side-door. I don't know who was the more startled, Victor or the young man who opened it, for he was dressed in full SS uniform – barely ten years after the war, when every outward sign of Nazism was banned. The young man slammed the door in Victor's face, and we heard his heavy top-boots thundering up the stairs. We looked for an inn elsewhere.

The spa doctor allowed us very few long drives, but we had to take one to Salzburg. Anyone who has been there will bring away memories of its architecture, its atmosphere and its beautiful setting; but I guarantee that no one will have a memory as bizarre as ours. As we explored the city streets we came upon a huge ironmonger's shop of extraordinary allure. Remember, it was quite soon after the war; England was taking a long time to recover; Austria had been neutral, so its economy had been relatively unaffected. We were like children goggling over an unaccustomed spread of goodies, but our allowance of foreign exchange was so small that we could afford to buy only one item – and the object which caught our fancy was a lavatory brush. Believe it or not, we had never seen a brush inside a plastic holder, such as millions of British homes possess today. So we carried it off in triumph, and, through my *House & Garden* connections, we lent it to a manufacturer to copy. The rest, as they say, is history.

8

When Victor and I came together again after thirteen years he laid down one guide-line for our relationship, saying, 'We are going to do everything together. There will be things I want to do which won't interest you, and vice versa, but we are going to do them together just the same.' This was put to the test as far as I was concerned when Victor took me off to a shooting-range somewhere on the outskirts of London. He was a very good shot and extremely keen. He had done practice shooting with the London Metropolitan Police. Who but Victor would have dreamt that up? There was a small club hut at this shooting-range, and a stretch of ground on which men lay flat on their stomachs and fired at targets. This went on for a long time. Not knowing what I was in for I hadn't brought a book, but I promised myself to bring one next time. But 'next time' never came, because that posture and those movements gave him a painful shoulder, which made us plan spa treatment, preferably in an unknown country. This led us to Bulgaria.

Shortly before I left *Vogue* I had had a letter, written in perfect English, ostensibly from a Dr Tzonchev of Plovdiv – but actually written by his wife, as I learnt later. It said that he wanted to give his wife a birthday present, and that some back numbers of *Vogue* would be a source of great pleasure. I sent off a packet and we started a correspondence, during which we asked Dr Tzonchev whether there were spas in Bulgaria. We were told that the Romans had discovered hot-water springs there, as they did all over Europe, and that the one most suitable for Victor was at

Kyustendil, near the Yugoslav border. There was no hotel, but he thought he could find us a place – which turned out to be the miners' rest home: Bulgaria followed the example of the Soviet Union in providing specific treatment for workers' health problems, and accommodation for their families. We were given a bed-sitting room with a small balcony, and were charged a modest hotel price, with the treatment free. A bowl of fresh fruit was brought up every day. We took our meals in the communal dining-room, and excellent meals they were. It was September, the season for fruit and vegetables. I have never tasted such delicious tomatoes, red, pink and yellow.

We were something of a curiosity in the little town, where they had never seen a foreigner. People came up to us in the street, trying every possible language; and Victor was able to cope with it all because Bulgarian is very similar to Russian and he had a smattering of other tongues. One excited man rushed up to say, 'I would like you to know that I am a follower of your Bernard Shaw. I, too, am a vegetarian.'

People were kind and generous to a touchingly naïve extent, because they had not yet been blighted by tourism. One day in the little park, when we were listening to the band and watching men and women of every age getting up from their seats to join hands in their national dance, a man sitting on our bench began talking to Victor. Asked about pensions, Victor told him that he had a State pension but had started his business too late in life for an industrial pension plan. Our neighbour then said it must be very difficult for us to manage. Victor reassured him, but to no avail. The man finally put his hand in his pocket, drew out a pile of notes and held it out saying, 'Help yourself.' Of course Victor refused, thanking him warmly. But our neighbour was still determined to help us. He asked where we would be staying in Sofia, and said that he would tell his son and daughter – university students – to show us the sights, which they did.

At the rest home we got to know a doctor who had brought his mother for treatment. He had a little car, was at a loose end, and took us for several drives. When doctors qualified in Bulgaria they had to spend the first three or four years practising in whatever part of the country they were sent to. Young doctors had been taking up any work which enabled them to live in Sofia, when the medical skills they had gained at the country's expense were badly needed in remote areas. This doctor had been sent to a mountainous region where he had been called to a shepherd's hut. He told us, 'For the first time in my life I put my stethoscope on a heart which had been beating for more than a hundred years.' Never before had the shepherd called a doctor, and he was reassured that the ailment was slight and that he could get up for a meal, which the doctor was invited to share. The family round the table consisted of his great-grandfather patient, a son in his seventies, a grandson in his forties, a teenage great-grandson and sundry women to match. They were all in perfect health, living several thousand feet up, entirely on the products of their sheep: milk and the yoghurt made from it; lamb and mutton; wool, woven and knitted; and sheepskin coats.

Perhaps it was the three hundred years of Turkish occupation that sowed the seeds of Eastern-style hospitality in Bulgaria. It was very charming, but at times rather overwhelming, as on a day when we stood by a garden fence to watch the owners pick fruit from their trees. The next thing we knew was a huge box of apples being passed over the fence to us. Victor protested that it was more than we could carry and that the rest home gave us fruit every day. Obviously disappointed, the donors whittled down their gift to a few kilos. The climax of our special-visitor status came on the public holiday that celebrated the achievement of St Cyril and St Methodius, to whom is attributed the creation of the Cyrillic alphabet in the ninth century. Schools and universities are specially concerned in the event, but the general population plays its part and, in Kyustendil, it took the form of a march past the podium (on which we were established alongside the town dignitaries) by a procession of singing, cheering citizens, carrying large bouquets which they flung at us with all their might as they went by.

When our three-week cure was finished we went to Plovdiv, the second city of Bulgaria, to meet the Tzonchevs, and stayed at a newly built hotel called the Trimontium, Plovdiv being built on three hills. Our bathroom was well appointed but had the curious feature of providing only cold water in the shower and basin while that in the WC was steaming hot. When we stayed again in the hotel seven years later, nothing had changed.

Ivan and Maria Tzonchev took us one day to the Rhodope Mountains, to lunch with a family who held the doctor in high regard. His skill had saved the life of one of two brothers, who lived together with their wives and their mother. We sat down to a huge meal, our hosts refusing to eat with us but standing behind our chairs and heaping food on to our plates. Being in the mountains, thickly sprinkled with flowers, Victor was inspired to ask whether they kept bees. Their faces lit up. Oh yes! Unfortunately only the old mother liked honey, so they had barrels of it in the cellar. Before we knew where we were, soup plates brimming with honey were placed in front of us, and we were invited to eat it with a spoon.

Later, strolling along a mountain path, we came on a solitary house, outside which a pretty girl was on the look-out. Maria began talking to her and heard that the daughter of the house was getting married and they were expecting relatives. Maria recognized them to be Turkish-Bulgarians, and knew that the birth of a girl set the mother and aunts to work, weaving household textiles for her dowry. So she asked whether we might see this wonderful pile of fabrics – which was indeed a replica of a display in a local folk museum. Other pieces of weaving lay apart from the dowry and I asked Maria whether it might be possible to buy something. Oh no! They never sold their work. So what were they going to do with that material? It was not a part of the dowry, and Maria's friends wanted to take some Bulgarian work back to England. Well, perhaps they could spare one metre. But I wanted more, so a reverse type of bargaining began and the yardage was finally pushed up to 2 metres. I still have those red and green cushion covers, their brilliance unfortunately faded – as always happens with vegetable dyes.

Bulgaria is a beautiful, interesting country whose prosperity – at least in the sixties – lies in the countryside rather than the towns. It has a fine geographical recipe for agricultural success: wide valleys protected by high mountains, with rivers running through them which can be harnessed for irrigation. Like the Russians, they had a flourishing private-plot economy; and, in the markets, their products were grouped together and of greater diversity, higher quality and price than the products of the State farms. When it became known that we were farmers, we were taken to see these farms. One of them was much the size of our own. We both had dairy herds and arable crops, and we had a pig section, too. However, there were twenty workers on their farm as against four on ours. Of course we were more highly mechanized, but agriculture in communist countries was, like all businesses, wildly overstaffed. It was a lovely throwback to my childhood to see apples, pears and plums being picked from high trees by people perched on ladders; but, on a second visit, seven years later, those trees had already been replaced by dwarf types whose fruit could be picked from the ground.

Besides its landscape, Bulgaria possesses fine architectural and archaeological treasures. We visited two great monasteries, Rila and Bachkovo; the medieval town of Turnovo; the Black Sea peninsula of Nessebur, thick with churches of the sixth and seventh centuries; and the underground Thracian tomb at Kazanluk, into which only two visitors were allowed at once, so that no crowding could damage the fragile murals. Christianity came very early to Bulgaria, but, under the Turkish occupation, the only churches permitted to be built were single storey, of a style indistinguishable from a barn. So the Bulgarians responded by excavating a whole underground area which they decorated with all the richness of the most cherished Orthodox church. Where, with us, a crypt is simple, austere and rather dark, in Bulgaria it is brilliant with frescoes, iconostases and gilded ironwork.

Bulgaria also possesses two groups of the most remarkable gold treasures in the world. One, in a Plovdiv museum, was displayed in a rickety case that could have been dismantled in minutes; and we were alone in the room during our visit. It consists of rhytons (large jugs), their handles modelled in the form of deer; beakers; and a great bowl, ornamented with row upon row of Negro heads. It is thought that its owners buried it before some invasion but never lived to retrieve it. The other treasure is in the crypt of the church of Santa Sophia in Sofia, whose construction is much heavier and its design simpler. We were told that a visitor to a village noticed a rather unusual vessel being used for the farm animals' drinking water. The villagers said that they had come across it when digging their land, that it was so heavy that they had cut a piece off before they could lift it, but it never tarnished and was perfect for the job. When the visitor returned to Sofia he alerted the archaeological department, who pounced on the village, arrested the inhabitants, and rounded up the whole cache, which was scattered among the cottages.

On our second visit to Bulgaria in 1968 we stayed in a small clinic in Hissar. It had been a Roman settlement – there again, they had found hot springs – and a massive Roman arch straddled the road into the little town. Wandering around, we came upon a group of charming cottages, which Victor was photographing when a man appeared, asked who we were and what we were doing, and made a furious attack on us: foreigners who would take home photographs of tumbledown buildings as representative of Bulgaria. Why were we not photographing the clinic – a modern building in which medical work was carried out? Victor explained that the clinic looked like any other modern building, while the cottages were picturesque and unusual. The man left us angrily and went to the clinic, demanding that we should be thrown out. He was the Communist Party leader of the area, but the clinic bravely refused to obey him.

It was a minor but unpleasant feature of communist regimes that its members attempted to stop any action of which they disapproved. In Leningrad we, with Misha and our friend Alexander Titov, were photographing Chesme Church – a delicious pink-and-white birthday-cake of a building which stands in the middle of a large open space, with blocks of flats on its edges. The middle-aged man who appeared on the scene must have spotted us from afar. Here there was no question of 'foreigners', only three Russians and an anonymous woman, but our visitor pitched into us just as violently. Why were we photographing the church? Why didn't we photograph the blocks of flats? Misha and Alexander – both architects who had spent the last twenty years restoring their city's historic buildings – explained that the church had been restored with government money, on government instructions, and that it was therefore a proper subject for photography. Our visitor was unconvinced, but finally retreated, growling as he went.

9

Victor loved the United States, and I can understand why. He liked the self-made character of its culture, and felt that he would have done well in it – which was probably true. Its great variety and size emulated those of Russia, and made him feel at home. He knew the West and Middle West better than the East, and their informality appealed to him. It was said by friends in Arizona that in earlier days a man on horseback could ride up to any ranch; his horse would be fed and watered, he would sit down to a meal, and no one would ask where he had come from or where he was going. Much of that unquestioning friendliness remains, and is very engaging.

In 1955 Victor and I pulled off a coup. We were both due to make business trips to America and we managed to arrange for the dates to coincide. When our work was done we hoped to stay with friends of Victor's in Rhode Island, but they had booked a holiday in Hawaii at just that time. They told us, however, that we were very welcome to stay at their house, where we should have the services of their black couple, their chauffeur and car, and the company of their Labrador dog and Siamese cat.

One day our friends' chauffeur suggested that we should drive up the Mohawk Trail – crowded in summer, but empty in March. A dusting of snow lay on what we would call villages but which Americans call townships. Indeed, outside each one, a road sign announced, *You are entering an All-American township*, and then gave the name and the date when it was founded (all in the eighteenth century), and the population – just a thousand or two. We were struck by the fact that there was not a fence or a wall to be seen. The houses and gardens were set out on the grass like a toy-town spread on the carpet by a child, and always there was a little church with a steeple. I asked the chauffeur, 'All-American? I thought we were in America!' He said that the phrase meant that there was no crime.

For one visit to Arizona we chose March, in order to see the desert bloom. It is an astonishing sight. After months in which green and sand-brown are the only colours, red, yellow, purple and white miraculously appear, without benefit of rain. The tall saguaro cactuses sprout succulent white flowers like water-lilies; scarlet plumes wave at the tips of cactus stems; carpets of tiny purple and white flowers cover the sand. One stroll was along a narrow, dry watercourse left by the heavy rains of the fall. I was in front. I told Victor to step quietly – as I did – on to the bank above. Lying a few feet ahead was a rattlesnake, asleep in the sun. Victor wanted to kill it with his tripod, but I said it had more right to be there than we had. Also I thought it would be a foolish risk.

In the autumn of 1965 we had left the farm and settled in at Gloucester Place Mews. It had been a difficult year, and we had a great urge to get away from it all. Victor knew that I was strongly drawn to Latin America, which he had never visited; so he went off to a shipping company in the City and booked a cabin on a Swedish cargo boat bound for Chile. In those days shipping companies often ran cargo boats with three or four passenger cabins. In early December we went to Antwerp to catch our boat, which was arriving from Stockholm.

It was a fabulous voyage. We first touched land in Venezuela, at La Guaira, the port of Caracas, a city that lies in an immensely long, deep valley, behind the coast. We went up the mountain-side in a cable-car and looked down on the sea below. In dramatic contrast to the brilliant colours of the tropics we saw huge soot-black butterflies with their wings stretched across the window of the terminus hut. As evening came on, the valley became a river of light from the spreading streets and houses.

Our boat called at Maracaibo and Barranquilla, ports along the Caribbean coast where we were due either to deliver or pick up goods: of course the cargo was everything and the passengers nothing – commercially speaking. At each port a notice was put up saying the hour at which the boat would sail – and sail it would, whether or not passengers had returned from their shore trip. The most interesting port was Cartagena, where the conquistadores assembled their stolen treasures to be shipped to Spain. The narrow entrance to its huge harbour made it easy to defend from invaders. There were whole streets of Spanish-Colonial buildings and, behind the town, the ground rose steeply to a fort from which there was a fine view of the whole scene. Luckily the captain had plenty of goods to handle, so we had several hours on shore.

The first officer constantly warned us to take nothing of value when we went ashore, because stealing, in those parts, had reached a level of artistry unknown in Europe. He told us of passengers who had gone ashore after one of his admonitions and returned saying that no one had come near them. One man, when asked 'Weren't you wearing sun-glasses?' put his hand to his nose and said, 'Yes'. They were no longer there. Earrings can be removed from ears, unfelt, and one of our passengers had his wrist-watch taken – again without being aware of anyone near.

We arrived in Callao, the port of Lima, on New Year's Eve and, in the city itself, were put in touch with a lady who had turned her family house into rented flats. As we proposed to stay for three months it was both cheaper and much more interesting to have our own place than to be in a hotel. Judging from old photographs, Lima was one of the most beautiful cities in the world even in the early years of this century. Its Spanish-Colonial domestic architecture, and its many churches, were of the seventeenth and eighteenth centuries. By the time of our arrival only four of the great houses were still standing and these had been taken over by ministries. All but a handful of churches had been demolished. High blocks of no architectural value had sprung up. Lima itself would have been boring if it had not been for three remarkable private collections – all of which the owners were prepared to show to visitors who had an introduction from a well-known citizen. Our landlady was such a one.

The most spectacular of all was a collection of Inca treasures, at

146

the home of its owner, Mujica Gallo, outside the city. We arrived at this palatial house at cocktail time, and joined a group in a room that housed a gigantic ironwood table – black, and so heavy that it had taken ten men to carry it in. In a warm climate, which suggests the long evenings of summer, it is surprising to find – when you are near the Equator – that the light fades early; and it was dark by the time our host led us into the garden and unlocked a trapdoor from which stairs sloped down to the underground museum. Here, marvellous objects were splendidly displayed, and we returned later to photograph them. Our host told us that, because he was known to be leaving his collection to the City of Lima, he was the first to be shown objects found in the archaeological digging that went on all the time. The early settlements were on the sea, where the sands are soft and – as the rainfall is around an inch a year – bone dry, so that the objects found are in perfect condition.

Another collector was descended from a titled Spanish-American family. He specialized in all the things which belonged to that culture: furniture, pictures, costumes, china, silver, and ornaments of all kinds. An entire table was covered with exquisite shoes of brocade and many-coloured silks. His American-English was fluent, but certain nuances escaped him, as with the charming remark, 'My father was a banker because he had a bank. And he was a miner because he had a mine.' He, also, was bequeathing his collection to the city and was the first to be offered items of its period.

The third collection belonged to a Japanese businessman who had spent most of his life in Peru and was fascinated by its ancient textiles. He told us that, as the people of Inca times had no written language, they used textiles to tell the story of their lives. Those living on the coast were fishermen, so their boats, and the fish they caught, figured largely. Most remarkable are those showing faces and bodies in so clinically accurate a way that doctors can diagnose the diseases from which they were suffering.

We spent three months in Peru, and made a series of expeditions up and down the coast and into the Andes. These last had each to be made separately, from Lima, as there was virtually no communication between Andean towns; and this had the drawback that, each time, we went from sea-level to 10,000 feet or more. After a few days one's body becomes accustomed to the altitude, but at the next expedition one starts again from scratch. Our first experience was a train journey to Huancayo, celebrated for its Sunday market. It lasted several hours, the route zigzagging up the mountains in a series of huge hairpin bends, to a pass at 11,000 feet. It is the highest railroad in the world. At the little hotel we climbed the stairs very slowly, resting every few steps. At dinner we could eat only the first course, and we had been warned to drink no alcohol.

The Sunday market was all the more fascinating because it was a purely Indian event. The stalls were piled with things that they would wear or use in their homes. It was clear that every woman had to have a hat; and those from different villages wore different styles, always brimmed. Even the babies, slung on their mothers' backs, wore tiny brimmed hats. Those babies, carried everywhere in the folds of their mothers' ponchos, never appeared to struggle or cry. We were told that they were drugged by their mothers' milk, for it is an Indian habit to dull the hardship of life by chewing coca leaves, the source of cocaine.

While Western physique has to adjust to altitudes, the Indians of the Andes are equipped with appropriate hearts, lungs and digestive systems. We often saw Indians trotting beside small herds of llamas when we could not have run a step. Until the Spanish brought in horses, Peru did not possess an animal that could be ridden, so the only way to go from place to place was to walk or run. At its height, the Inca empire included the whole of what are now Ecuador, Peru, Bolivia and part of Chile, yet the government in the capital, Cuzco, knew what was happening in every part of their empire. Men must have covered hundreds of miles, in stages, in the way horses were used in Europe before the arrival of cars. They would have been carrying elaborate cat's-cradles of knotted string, which recorded the harvest gathered in different regions and provided treasury records. They are called *quipus*. Some are in the museums, and no one has been able to translate the messages they conveyed. However, while most lowlanders can adjust to altitudes, the reverse is not true. Andean

Indians, coming down to the coast in search of an easier life, are likely to fall ill with pneumonia and respiratory diseases.

Under the Incas the nation's wealth was divided into three parts: one for the royal family, one for the priests and one for the people. I don't know whether the priests' portion was used in social welfare causes, but the Incas' was available to help out any region or family that had been hard hit by harvest loss, disease or accident. Widows and orphans were cared for. When the Spaniards conquered Peru they took over this system, but adapted it disastrously, directing a third to the government in Madrid, a third to the Vatican, and a third to remain in Peru – of which very little reached the Indians. To this day their ownership of land is minimal, and that land is seldom fertile. We watched Indians trying to cultivate a piece of mountainside so steep that they had to secure themselves from falling by waist-ropes pegged to the ground.

Our next Andean expedition was to Ayacucho – later, notorious as an area dominated by Shining Path guerrillas, but then a peaceful and charming small town, with several magnificent Spanish-Colonial churches. Altars are their most impressive feature; not only at the east end but in the small chapels which line both sides; and the sculptures and ornamentation rise up in tiers almost to the roof. Sometimes the figures are actually clothed in garments and everything glitters with gold. Frequently doors of painted wood hide the figures above the main altar, to be opened only on some appropriate date in the religious calendar. For several days Victor and I roamed through the little town, and we never met any kind of threat or confrontation. The only alarming moments were before touchdown on the airfield. Owing to the air currents, approaching planes have almost to strike the mountainside far below and then, as it were, climb up like a fly climbing a wall.

We flew south to Arequipa, a handsome Spanish-Colonial city, second in size to Lima and on a comparatively low range of the Andes, only 5,000 feet up. On the outskirts we went into a small village church where Victor wanted to photograph the altar. A large box in the form of a cross stood in the way, but he couldn't shift it. Then we saw a slot at the top. It was a giant collection-box. 'Oh yes,' said friends. 'And every so often it would be emptied, and a cheque for the whole sum sent to Rome.' This was a humble little church in a poor area. The Inca empire was more truly civilized than that of its Spanish destroyers.

The excitement of that flight was looking down on the remarkable Nazca 'lines', drawn on the ground below but visible only from the air. There are endless arguments about the date and the significance of these mysterious patterns, which cover miles of the flat strip of land that lies between the sea and the mountains. I know of no other decorative work, on a large scale, that is invisible at ground level. Deep marks on the earth's surface – such as archaeological sites, or the trenches of the 1914–18 war – are invisible from the ground but clear as a map from the air; but those, in their day, were dug for use, while the Nazca 'lines' are pure decoration.

The most thrilling experience of our three-month stay in Peru was the visit to Cuzco and its surroundings, and on to Macchu-Picchu. Cuzco was of course the Inca capital, and a number of structures from that time remain. They are built from large blocks of stone, of varied sizes and shapes, fitted together without mortar, and with such precision that it is literally impossible to insert a knife between them. Only for some very special structure have blocks of stone been carefully fashioned to an exact size, and laid in straight rows. On the hills above there are the remains of the huge fortress of Sacsayhuaman. These and other Inca structures are ruins only because later generations pilfered them for their own buildings, as was the case with England's ruined abbeys.

The journey to Macchu-Picchu was an experience in itself. The three-coach train trundled along the narrow valley which was almost filled by the River Urubamba. So close was the rail-track that spray from its waters was blown against the windows. After some three hours we left the train for a coach which climbed the hairpin bends on the road to Macchu-Picchu. These extraordinary remains, in their spectacular setting, are so familiar that it is needless for me to describe them. But something which the usual photographs cannot show is the centrepiece of the complex, perched at its highest point – the *intihuatana*, a huge block of stone, carved to make coils rising in an erection resembling a phallus, or a rearing cobra. The name means 'hitching post of the sun'. As in many religions, the sun was worshipped and, as the days grew shorter, the Indians feared that it was disappearing. However, the priests, who had some knowledge of astronomy, knew better. At the winter solstice they turned that knowledge into religious power by casting a lasso over the 'hitching post', to rein in the sun. And – by a miracle, as it seemed – it came slowly back to illuminate the people's lives and ripen their crops.

With a foresight for which we thanked our lucky stars, we had booked a room for the night in the only inhabited building on the site – a little hotel, in which there were only two other visitors. The day-trippers left for their train in mid-afternoon and another group arrived next mid-morning, so for hours on end we roamed the terraces alone. And surely that is the most alarming thing about the growth of tourism: that it is now almost imposs-ible to be alone. I find it very difficult, in a crowd, to enjoy looking at buildings or at pictures. You see them, but you don't feel them; and an experience such as that of Macchu-Picchu demands emptiness and silence. My father used to quote the story that George Borrow (I think) told against himself. He had encountered a solitary gypsy woman at the top of a mountain, and held forth about the beauties of the scene while she stood in silence. When he remarked on her apparent indifference, she replied, 'A disn't blither. A jist enjiys it.' I think they would both have enjoyed it more if they had been alone.

One of our expeditions was to the Amazon jungle. A United States company, Letourneau, which specialized in heavy equip-ment, got a concession from the Peruvian Government to de-velop a large area for cattle rearing. Peru has comparatively little land suitable for crops, let alone for ranching. The company was to create a small airport and a link-road with the nearest high-way, as well as to clear the jungle. A small community of Amer-icans worked on the project; one family had gone to the United States for their vacation and we were lent their house.

In this great clearing in what would now be called the 'rain forest', one of the staff drove us around in a jeep. We got out on a rise which looked over the 'ranch' and were told that it comprised hundreds of cattle. However, we had only a few glimpses of the white coat of a Charollais showing above the scrub. The bull-dozers which were used to clear the jungle were so big that a man could stand upright inside the hub of a wheel; but, within weeks, the scrub would spring up again. It had to be cleared two or three times a year, if cattle were to be raised, and we were not surprised to hear, a few years later, that the whole project had been abandoned. The disastrous clearing of the rain forest in Brazil is always described as permanent destruction, and the promotion of cattle-ranching as being the main objective: which makes me wonder why the Peruvian experience of losing forest trees, failing to gain grazing land, and being left with useless scrub, is not deterring the developers of Brazil.

Insects were plentiful in the Amazon jungle – particularly ants, indoors and out. We were specially interested in a colony of large leaf-cutting ants that were on the march between their home and the manager's garden. He told us that the ants' target was one particular tree, and that they would carry on till they had stripped it bare. We watched them on their miniature highway, with one column going out empty-handed and the other returning, each carrying a large piece of leaf, held aloft like a sail. One late afternoon the piled-up clouds turned black and the first raindrops fell. A tropical storm was about to break. What about the ants? we thought. They will all be drowned. But the highway was deserted; somehow they sensed the danger and stayed home. Then came a remarkable phenomenon: scattered about the sky, against the clouds, were sections of rainbows – not part of any arc but at different angles. The rain poured down, and a nearby tributary of the Amazon rose 24 feet in the night.

I cannot take leave of Latin America without mention of the barriadas, the appalling slums that surround the cities. They are not 'slums' in the Western sense of run-down, dilapidated build-ings; they have nothing that could be called a building at all. They are simply a conglomeration of shacks, thrown together out of material of every kind, with no sanitation, no electricity, and only standpipes of water at intervals. Open sewers run through them. Adults and children swarm everywhere. Few have a settled job. They live by begging, stealing and selling any odds and ends they have come by. If anyone needs to be convinced of the need for controlling population growth, they should visit a barriada.

After three wonderful months in Peru we boarded a boat of the same Swedish Line at Callao. We were returning in style, having been assigned the owner's cabin: positively a suite, with sitting-room and bunk-room, and sited all by itself up a stairway from the other cabins. We were given this privilege because they knew that we were going to give publicity to the voyage in features for which Victor had been taking photographs and I taking notes. We were grateful for the peace and space the owner's cabin gave us to sort these out on the return journey; and we had the pleasure of playing host to the ship's officers and our fellow-passengers by inviting them to drinks.

10

I have described elsewhere the party of Indian tourists we met on a night train between Leningrad and Moscow during our first visit to Russia. Swami Iyer (the one who said he would call on Victor's son working in Coimbatore) wrote to Victor from time to time. While we were still in our first flat in Ennismore Gardens a letter came from Swami, telling us that his sons were coming to London to buy equipment for their factory, and 'I have told them that you and Mrs will be father and mother to them.' We need not have been apprehensive about this role. Two very self-assured young men turned up, carrying government credits for large sums, and obviously having no need of parents. Later, hearing of our travels and photography in Peru, Swami suggested that we visit India, saying that we could stay in his son's house in Madras, and with other relatives around the country.

It was an exciting idea. We decided to go in December 1970, beginning with Sri Lanka, crossing to Madras, visiting the famous places of the south, and then working our way up to Delhi. We became good friends with the director of the Indian Tourist Office and she introduced us to the high commissioner's department, which would apply for the special permits needed to take in photographic equipment and film for a ten-week visit. Months went by. Frequent reminders brought no results, so we finally told them we were leaving for Sri Lanka. 'We will cable for the papers to be sent to you there,' they said. Nothing came, and we arrived paperless in Madras. But first, Sri Lanka.

Colombo is not an interesting city for visitors, but has beautiful environs, both coast and mountains. After a few days there we hired a car and a driver, and set off on a tour which took in Kandy, Sigiriya, Polonnaruwa and Anuradhapura. On the way to Kandy our driver drew up at the side of the road for us to see the memorial garden to the former prime minister, Mr Bandaraniaka. Before an election he had made promises to the Buddhists – and had not honoured them. So the head of the hierarchy ordered a monk to assassinate him. They were arrested; the monk was executed, his superior dying in prison. This was the more astonishing because Sri Lankans were the gentlest, kindest people we had ever encountered. Indeed we thought that if those qualities sprang from Buddhism, the world had better turn Buddhist. I remembered that in his book *Seven Years in Tibet* Heinrich Harrer described building workmen examining every spadeful of earth, in case a worm had been injured. Yet, as with other religions, Buddhism is capable of strange anomalies: the priests of a religion that forbade harming a worm were prepared to kill a human being; and, a few months after our visit, civil war broke out, and Sri Lanka has been a killing-field ever since.

We loved the country and, just as Peru had been our first experience of the tropics, with its strange new trees and flowers, birds and butterflies, so Sri Lanka was our first experience of the Buddhist sculpture and architecture we were to see in India. Polonnaruwa, with its statue of the sleeping Buddha stretched out along a rocky hillside, remains one of the greatest; and there are few moments which can give the thrill of standing on top of the huge rock of Sigiriya.

From Colombo we flew to Madras. And, such was our faith that the high commissioner's instructions would have reached the airport officials, that we confidently produced our photographic equipment – only to have the greater part of it confiscated. It was a disconcerting beginning to our working trip. But Swami said that he would get the help of a retired travel agent to find our permit, so he and Victor spent the best part of three days going from one office to another in search of the papers. They arrived at the desk of a man who said he knew nothing about them and was very busy. The agent asked if he might search: and there were the ones we needed, dated weeks earlier, and giving a clearance on everything we had brought. 'Can we take these papers away?' he asked. 'Oh no.' They had to be countersigned by some higher official. 'And can he do it now?' 'He won't be back till the end of the week.' So we had to leave Madras without them, for our first photographic venture at Mahabalipuram – luckily not far off, and luckily, too, that Swami could collect the equipment and films and bring them out to us. It is said that Britain is to blame for giving India its bureaucratic system, but India has developed the process with enthusiasm.

Swami's son and nephew, who were in business together, had built two houses, with a roadway between them and a communal garden at the back. We stayed, with Swami, in his son's house. His grandchildren went to a kindergarten run by Catholic nuns. As the family were high-caste Brahmins, I ventured to ask their mother if religion had any part in their schooling. Oh no, she said; the nuns understood the position; they were long-standing settlers in Madras, and had never attempted to convert anybody. This Brahmin family was actually proud that their little boy had been chosen to represent the baby Jesus in the Nativity play being performed that Christmas.

There is nothing that gives so much insight into differing national habits as staying in private houses, when abroad. We stayed in four such houses in India and, in each one, learnt something new about Indian life and attitudes. In the Madras house I quickly realized that I was the only woman who sat at table with the men. At first I thought that Swami's daughter-in-law was taking her meals with the children. Then one evening a young couple were invited to dinner, and the nephew and his wife came over from the house next door – and still I was the only woman at the dinner table. After the meal I glanced through the kitchen door – and there were the three young women, dressed in their finest saris, sitting on the floor, eating the re-mains of our meal. I was deeply embarrassed but unable to say or do anything. That was their accepted custom.

Swami told us that we could stay with his three daughters as we travelled north. 'But I thought you only had one daughter?' 'Well, yes, that's true. But my brother's daughters are my daugh-ters and my daughter is his daughter.' The extended family is alive and well in India. We stayed with Swami himself at his ancestral home in a village in Kerala, with his brother's house next door. The village, dating from the eighteenth century, was peaceful and orderly, with very little traffic. In Swami's brother's house we were shown an upstairs, windowless room, and were told that, in earlier days, the women of the household spent their menstrual periods there, unable to see or be seen. Kerala feels superior to other states in that almost 100 per cent of its population is literate, with a high proportion of university graduates. Nevertheless these qualified doctors, lawyers and accountants want to work only in Kerala, and the state cannot absorb them all.

The almost universal knowledge of the English language among educated people is Britain's most valuable bequest to India. Indian friends going on holiday in another state had learnt the rudiments of its language, but when they tried to use it to ask the way, the policeman shouted, 'For goodness' sake! Don't any of you speak English?' But there can be embarrassments to the English visitor, because Indian-English has developed its own pronunciations and expressions. Late one evening the door of our room in a guest-house was flung open and two almost identical heads appeared, one above the other: they were the brother-managers. One mouth opened, saying 'Betty? Betty?' We had no answer. 'Betty? Betty?' I managed a reply, 'No Betty, thank you.' 'What on earth were you talking about?' asked Victor. 'They were asking whether we wanted tea in bed.'

The family we stayed with in Bangalore had a handsome daughter who had just graduated from the university. It was now the proper time for her to marry, and her parents were embarking on the lengthy preliminaries. Almost all Indian marriages are arranged; it is rare for young people to take marriage into their own hands. Advertisements are published in the local papers, describing the prospective bride or bridegroom, with details of their looks, age and education. A light skin is desirable, and so is a university degree, even for a bride, and even though few women work after marriage. Good photographs were needed, to be shown to the parents of the prospective spouse. So it was explained to us that, on the way out to a restaurant dinner, we should be calling at a photographer's studio. A careful choice had been made of the sari the girl should wear for the occasion. It was light brown with a gold border which, they felt, gave the right impression of beauty that was dignified and mature, rather than flashy.

When it comes to conversations between parents, the two most important subjects are horoscopes and money. A record is always kept of the exact hour of birth, from which a horoscope is drawn up. This is a kind of testimonial on which everything depends. No responsible parent would be tempted by rank or wealth to overlook unpropitious signs when two horoscopes are compared. It is firmly believed that a successful marriage is impossible between those whose horoscopes are at odds.

When we reached Delhi we spent an evening with Swami's niece and her husband, who was a high-ranking civil servant. After dinner she and I talked in one corner of the room while he and Victor talked in another; but at least we had all dined together. Mrs Iyer said that, while staying with her relatives, I would have noticed how much time they and their servants spent in grinding spices. She bought her spices ready-ground, to give more time for working with a blood-donor association. Altogether she was far more sophisticated than her 'sisters'; so I was all the more taken aback when, in reference to the Vietnam war, she said, 'Oh, Mrs Kennett, what wicked people the Vietnamese must be!' When I asked why she thought so, she replied that Hindus believed that the lives of individuals and nations were determined, for better or worse, by their previous actions. 'In Vietnam there has been one war after another. What wicked people they must be!' When I tried to argue that wars were not necessarily started by the country in which they were fought, I was met by the brick wall of her faith.

India is so vast, and so packed with wonders, that those who start in Delhi may never reach the south. But, starting there, we saw Mahabalipuram, Kancheepuram, Tanjore and Madurai – all marvellous, but the first, perhaps, the finest of all. It is on the coast, and one of its temples is actually on the shore, where the breakers of the Indian Ocean come rolling in. There is an astonishing sculptural frieze – a procession with elephants – stretching for yards along a rock surface. The place – hardly more than a village – is magical and remote. But on our second visit it was invaded by a German tourist group, travelling in an overland bus that had served as a mobile hotel all the way from Europe. Its three decks contained bunks, wash-places, eating space, and housed about twenty passengers. They were spending a night at Mahabalipuram (usually they travelled non-stop, with drivers working in shifts); and several of them scuttled into the little hotel, understandably seeking a night in a stationary bed.

Kancheepuram not only has beautiful temples but a flourishing hand-woven silk industry, housed in family homes built round large open courtyards. It is a traditional craft, carried on from generation to generation. In complete contrast to factory line-up, the workers sit outside their doors, weaving their own length of silk, at their own speed, in a lovely range of colours. I bought lengths in moss green and turquoise; and Victor had an orange shirt, made in a day.

Among all the wonderful things we saw during our two long visits to India – Jaipur, and the exquisite palace of Amber; the Buddhist stupa of Sanchi; the 15 square kilometres of Vijayanagar ruins at Hampi – two places seen on that first visit stand out in my mind, possibly because they were remote, peaceful, untouched, and in which we were almost the only visitors. One was Mandu, which one could reach only by hiring a car at Indore, miles away. All along the high, flat mountain-top lie the sprawling remains of a great summer resort of Pathan rulers. There are half-ruined palaces, some with an upper storey from which projects an open area large as the deck of a liner, where the ladies of the court could take the air, undisturbed. One, perched on the edge of the ridge, had been built for Rani Roopmati, the beloved wife of Baz Bahadur. He had found her as a village maiden in the plain below; and although it was a lasting love-match, she never forgot her village life, and spent hours gazing down to where the silver streak of a river marked her home. The mosque could have held a thousand worshippers, such was the cavalcade that climbed each year into the cool mountain air, before the onset of summer heat. Now the only life is in a small village, and one guest-house with three bedrooms.

On our first morning in Mandu a young man presented himself. He had graduated from a college in the plain, had found no

159

work there, so had come home – where of course there was no work for him either, except as a guide to the rare visitor. We took him on, and we kept our car and its driver. On our last day there was a festival which the young man said would be celebrated under the light of a full moon. He duly came for us as darkness fell; and it was magical to stand on that high ridge and see a huge yellow moon hanging in the sky, on a level with our eyes. At first we walked on land empty except for the Moghul buildings, but then began to pass dimly lit shacks, from whose open doors came loud sounds of celebration. Suddenly the young man bolted into one of these and we heard a welcoming cry go up. We waited outside, thinking he would rejoin us, but he never came, and it was obvious that the group was far gone in drink. There were no lights except in the huts; there were no paths; we were at least a mile from the guest-house, and we hadn't looked to see where we were going. We felt rather uncomfortably lost. And then a figure loomed up – our driver. He had guessed that we might be abandoned; he knew that on such occasions no one could be relied on, for they were all drunk; so he had come to lead us back to the guest-house. We were grateful and impressed, and it was a pleasure to give him a special tip when we parted next day.

The other remote and peaceful place was Mount Abu. It also could be reached only by car. It is a mountain of three or four thousand feet which stands up in the plain of Rajasthan. On the top were the objects of our journey: three Jain temples. The Jains are a sect dating from centuries before the birth of Christ and still flourishing today. Unlike Hinduism, it has no gods, but reveres a long series of wise men called Tirthankaras. We went to the entrance of the temple complex, took off our shoes, and then the attendant examined the bag in which Victor carried his photographic equipment – a canvas fishing bag, piped with – what? 'Leather,' said the attendant. 'Surely not. Plastic?' suggested Victor. But leather it was; and, as the Jains will not allow in their sacred places anything that stems from the death of a living creature, the bag had to remain outside the shrine. But what about the equipment? Very simple. An old pillowcase was produced, into which all the gear was stuffed.

We were over the first hurdle; but there was a higher one. We were told to approach a long table set out in the open air, at which sat about eight impressive, elderly men. We exchanged bows, and I produced the precious paper we had got from a Ministry responsible for matters of national heritage, which stated that Victor was authorized to take photographs in any of such sites all over the country. On Mount Abu the paper was passed from hand to hand, and then their chief said, very politely, that he could see that we had such permission for sites under the Ministry's control, but that Jain temples were not in that category; they were under the control of the Jains themselves. We were stunned; we had come several hundred miles for this one purpose. We begged the Elders to grant our request, and held our breath while they debated the case. They agreed.

During three days' work no one came near us, no one watched our movements or interfered in any way – so different from the Hindu temples we had worked in, which were swarming with people, where priests and acolytes came up holding out their hands for alms and, if they didn't think it enough, cried out, 'You give this to the God?' Whatever the amount, one was pretty sure it would go into their own pockets.

Two of the Mount Abu temples were built in the thirteenth century, on the orders of two brothers, and are entirely of white marble which had to be brought on the backs of elephants from some distant quarry in the plain below. Their essential role in the enterprise is celebrated in one of the temples by a line of elephants, about five feet high, carved in the marble they had carried. The glory of these temples is the intricate carving which, though extremely elaborate, is never florid, but restrained and exquisite. Its tracery is detached from the main structure to an extent one would have thought impossible. When the brothers were invited to review the finished temples, they praised the stonemasons for their work, but asked them to try and detach the carving still further – saying that if they collected the marble dust they removed, they would be given its weight in silver. On a later visit the brothers gave their approval and carried out their promise, but urged still further refinements, for which the weight of the dust would be paid in gold. The result is that we saw small birds literally flying through the carving of capitals that crowned the pillars. The care the Jains have bestowed on the temples has kept these marvels as perfect as they were when the master carvers finally left them, 700 years ago, carrying their bags of well-earned silver and gold.

We had noticed that the young driver of our car to Mount Abu had a drawn, suffering expression, and we asked him what was the matter. He told us that he had constant pain in his stomach. His profession was very trying. He never knew when he would get a meal, and he often stayed overnight with his fares – as he would be doing with us – and slept curled up uncomfortably in the car. In the hotel we were given quarters with a spacious ante-room which would hold a bed; so Victor went to the management and asked for our driver to be put up there and allowed meals at our expense. In that way he got three nights' rest and regular food, and looked the better for it. When we returned to Ahmedabad we took him to a chemist, asked him to describe his symptoms and bought him the recommended medicine. To our astonishment, passing a taxi-rank, the drivers waved their arms and shouted excitedly. The news had got around.

In the caves of Ajanta – another marvel – we got into conversation with a man and a woman who had watched Victor's photographic operations with interest. They turned out to be the heads of a new initiative to encourage tourism. When they heard that our journey would end in Delhi, they gave us the name of a reliable developer of colour film and asked to be shown the results. This chance encounter was a very lucky one, for they were so impressed with Victor's photographs that they bought a large number; and, because they could pay for them only in non-transferable rupees, we were able to go to India for a second time, on the strength of that payment.

While visiting the magnificent temples of Madurai, on our first visit, Victor had become friendly with a local photographer who exhibited his work in our hotel. He processed some of Victor's black-and-white photographs, and they exchanged letters after our return to England. We owed him a debt of thanks for an introduction to a photographer in Agra – who went with us to the Taj Mahal and showed us a spot we should never have found for ourselves. The Taj is usually taken from a distance, showing the many basins of water that lead up to the building. This photographer took us up to the last basin, planting Victor on the very edge, almost pitching into the water, at which point the whole marvellous group of the central temple, its four surrounding turrets and the few formal trees, was completely reflected in the pool. When we showed the result to the India Tourist office in London, they said they had never seen a better shot.

When we planned a second visit in 1973 Victor decided to ask the Madurai photographer to travel with us, to help him. His health was deteriorating. He had never been able to photograph 'in passing', as it were, but always needed to stay a night so that he could choose the best light, and the best aspect of his subject-matter, which was basically architecture, interiors and landscape: static subjects he could study at his leisure. He realized that, in India, there were wonderful, rapidly changing scenes with which he could not cope; and he also felt the need for an assistant to carry the equipment, change the film and so on.

I had the interesting experience of being sent, as a patient, to a leper colony. I had developed a swollen, throbbing big toe: we were always walking barefoot in and around temples and could easily have picked up an infection. A doctor gave me a shot of penicillin and said that I should wear sandals rather than closed shoes, and that sandals with germ-proof soles were made at this colony, to which he gave me an introductory note. I was to keep my foot up for the taxi journey and at the colony. So off I went and lay on a bench there among the patients, while they made sandals whose rubber soles were specially manufactured in England.

We visited Varanasi (formerly Benares), famous for its burning ghats. Hindus believe that the water of the Ganges is holy, and that a funeral on its banks, and the scattering of ashes on its waters, will have a powerful influence on a future incarnation. Helpful relatives carry out these wishes. You pass a cyclist with a rather long plank projecting behind his back wheel; and see that, stretched out on it, is a corpse wrapped in gauze. We went out on the river at dawn, in a small launch, and saw more than ashes floating in the water. Yet all along the ghats there are people bathing ceremoniously in the sacred stream. In our hotel we got talking to a highly sophisticated Indian fashion designer who was making a name for himself in Paris. When asked what had brought him to Varanasi he replied, 'I want to take the water of the Ganges into my mouth.'

This hotel stood in a garden and could have been delightful. However, the proprietor was a remarkably unpleasant man, and when the swing-doors between kitchen and dining-room were pushed open, huge mottled rats rushed out and ran among the tables. Attached to our bill was one of those questionnaires that visitors usually ignore; but we filled ours in, rats and all, and when the proprietor ran into us, it was obvious that the dislike was mutual.

The hotel garden was the setting for a memorable experience. Two men were involved, one old and one young. The old man lay on his back on a thin mattress on the grass. He lay perfectly still; then his whole body, still stretched flat, rose in the air, turned over, and came down again on his back. The young man held a stance, with his body in a straight line, at an angle one would not have thought possible without his falling on his face. Then chairs with wooden arms were placed two feet or so from one another. The young man stood between them, with his hands on the arms – hands held down by servants – and turned a somersault through the air. We were sitting a few feet away, and there could have been no trickery. Some Indians are trained from childhood to control their bodies to an extent that Westerners find unbelievable.

We had intended to cover the wonderful complex of temples in Orissa. However, there was one of the periodic outbreaks of violence in that part of the country, with trains held up and passengers robbed and murdered, and it was ruled out as too dangerous. We consoled ourselves with Khajuraho, where the temples are rich with erotic sculptures.

So ended our last visit to India. If our five months had been five years we could not have covered all the marvels it contains. One wonders how India, and other countries with a wealth of treasures, will be able to protect and conserve them through passing centuries. Not everywhere are there devoted, rich guardians like the Jains of Mount Abu; and few buildings are made of stone as hard as the marble of their temples.

11

The India Tourist Office had been extremely helpful to us when we were planning our first visit to India. And of course, on our return, we took Victor's photographs to show to the director, who offered us the whole office to display them. We jumped at this opportunity, and set about getting big enlargements of the best black-and-white pictures of architecture and sculpture. We hung strings of small colour enlargements of the Indian life and landscape photographs.

The Indian high commissioner was asked to open the show, and I provided the names of those we wished to be invited to the opening. I listed the editors and art editors of publishing houses – books and magazines – with whom we had been in touch, and whose subject-matter included travel, architecture and interior decoration. Among these last was the art editor of Thames and Hudson. I showed him round and he was obviously impressed. I told him that Victor had made a large coverage of architecture in Leningrad, and that we were setting off in a few weeks time for our last photographic session. He was interested, and asked us to get in touch when we returned.

I must now go back to 1959 – our second visit to Leningrad. I had said to Victor that there was a book to be done there and, on our return, had invited Mr and Mrs Neurath, the founders of Thames and Hudson, to have a drink with us. At that time hardly anyone visited the USSR. Tourism did not exist, and so no photographs or articles were published about it. The Neuraths were interested and offered us an advance. However, we refused it, saying that we were still in full-time work, that many arrangements would have to be made, and that we would come back to them when we saw our way clear. A few years later, when Victor's brother Misha had used the old-boy network on our behalf (saying airily to the directors of palaces with whom he had worked on their restoration, 'You wouldn't mind if my brother from London took a few snaps?'), I called up Mrs Neurath with the glad news that we were beginning the work. I met with an icy response. The Neuraths had fled from Vienna in the late thirties; the building of the Berlin Wall finalized the division of Europe into East and West and they wanted no part in anything concerning the Soviet Union. It was a blow, but we went ahead during six visits to Leningrad and succeeded, with Misha's help, in covering all the palaces that could be visited at that time, and which had any rooms that warranted photography.

The Russian authorities showed a remarkable feeling for the preservation of their architectural heritage. They set about the total restoration of the great imperial palaces, and this sometimes meant the reconstruction of buildings wrecked by shells and bombs. The great homes of the nobility were also restored structurally, and two or three rooms kept furnished and decorated in their former manner, while the rest were used as offices, or clubs for the various professions – which had spendidly furnished public rooms. Restoration had proceeded on a scale, and with a dedication, that was unique. Misha was a member of a committee which, each year, sent the Ministry in Moscow detailed estimates of work needed to restore three damaged buildings. Only one would be chosen, but the work would then be carried out in its entirety. If the estimate included a floor inlaid with fifteen different woods, fifteen woods would be used. There was no skimping and saving. Where gold leaf was specified, it was used – not gold paint.

Misha had in fact been given the charge of sufficient gold leaf to cover the whole spire of Petropavlovsky Cathedral – that spire which is the symbol of St Petersburg, as the Eiffel Tower is of Paris. He told us that, when the work was finished, he had been invited to inspect it. He went up ladders inside the building until he reached a window in the spire, through which he stepped out on to a ladder stretching to the top: an incredible height, with absolutely nothing but a ladder to hold on to. He said in all sincerity that the view was so breathtaking that he didn't want to come down.

A vital factor in achieving the high quality of restoration was that architects in the eighteenth century designed not only the building but every detail of the interiors, down to the door-knobs. Their drawings had been kept in the museums and were taken out to be copied by the army of craftsmen assembled from all over the country, so that one now walks through rooms which look very much as they did when they were newly created. And this is a great improvement on their pre-revolutionary appear-ance, photographs of which show them cluttered with the stan-dard lamps and heavy armchairs of the late nineteenth and early twentieth centuries. Their original furnishings, pictures and ornaments had mostly been spirited to safety, before the siege, and were brought back to take their rightful place again, together with items of the period brought in from elsewhere. The result is a reconstruction triumph such as few countries can boast of.

Let me return to my conversation with the art editor of Thames and Hudson, at the exhibition of Victor's Indian photo-graphs. A few days later I was at my desk in Gloucester Place Mews when the telephone rang and a voice so deep that I took it to be a man's asked to speak to Mr Kennett. I said he was out, but I could take a message. The voice said, 'Tell him how much I admire his photograph of the sculpture on the stairs of the British Museum.' I asked who was speaking, and was told 'Mrs Neurath of Thames and Hudson'. I said I was afraid that she was calling the wrong Mr Kennett. (A well-known photographer, 'Kennet', had recently published a book on the Tutankhamun treasures.) Then I took a deep breath and asked her whether she remembered us, and our proposal for a book on the architecture of Leningrad. She did remember. I told her that we were on the verge of completing our project; also that we had recently met her art editor, who had said he would like to see us when we returned from Leningrad. Her response: 'The time to see you is before you go.'

So we lunched with her. Ten years had passed; the Berlin Wall was forgotten; and when we returned from Leningrad and showed our hoard of photographs Thames and Hudson were ready to go ahead with a book. They visualized it as consisting of photographs with captions, but I had different ideas. I felt that text was needed, that I could provide it, and I went to the V & A Library to research. I employed two graduates of the School of Slavonic Studies to read the relevant books published in Russian. We used to meet for a snack lunch and I would ask them what they had found. Day after day the answer was the same: practically nothing. Books published since the Revolution were mainly waffle. One of the crimes of communism was to impose a meaningless jargon form of writing where 'official' books were concerned. These never mentioned the owners of the palaces, the people whose taste and money had caused them to be built. They barely mentioned the architects, almost all of them foreign (Italian, French, German and Scottish), saying instead that they were built by serfs – no doubt the truth, but not the whole truth. When I put these researchers on to books published in an earlier period, they found a completely different approach and were able to give me plenty of notes.

The whole experience of preparing our book for publication was a delight. We were assigned an excellent editor, who became a good friend. The fact that I had been an editor myself made it much easier to understand her role and to respect her judgement. I presented the text of each section to her, she would come back with criticisms and I would rewrite (and retype – no word processors in those days) until she was satisfied. Work with the art editor went smoothly. My experience of dealing with photographs and layouts made it easy to pick good pictures and to gauge the length of captions needed; and years of proof-reading made that no problem for me either. At the Frankfurt Book Fair Thames and Hudson had arranged for three foreign editions of *The Palaces of Leningrad* – American, German and French.

It was as a spin-off from that book that a call came from Jacqueline Onassis, in New York. She said that she was editing the illustrated catalogue of a forthcoming exhibition of Russian costume at the Metropolitan Museum. She and the museum director were going to the USSR to choose clothes from their museums. She would be in London on her return journey, and would we come and have tea with her? The day fixed was the one before we were due to move house, with removers arriving at nine o'clock next morning. We turned up at her suite in the Ritz, tired and dishevelled. Victor had been complaining that he had not had a square meal for days so, when a trolley laden with food appeared, he quietly ate his way through a plate of smoked salmon sandwiches while she and I talked. Her main purpose was to invite me to write the introduction to the catalogue; and we discussed the form it should take, its length and the date of delivery. She said that she had come to us after looking through a range of books on Russian subjects, because she felt that ours gave the best idea of Russian social life in the eighteenth and nineteenth centuries – the period covered by the exhibition. I liked her decision that, apart from the introduction, there should be only short, factual accounts of each reign, prefacing the display of costumes of that period; and that, besides the captions describing the costumes shown, there should be apt quotations taken from contemporary writings. Mixed in with the costume illustrations, she planned to show portraits of the celebrities of the time and engravings of St Petersburg: and she chose a number of Victor's photographs of these subjects.

The only snag, from my point of view, was that Mrs Onassis wanted the copy in about four weeks time. We were in the chaos of moving house, and I should have to research into a fresh aspect of Russian life. I set out again for the V & A Library and, as I could not be sure I had got it right, I sent her some trial pages and she cabled OK. I then sent the whole piece a few days before the deadline, so that there would be time for alterations. It arrived at the New York publisher's office on a Saturday morning, not a likely time for mail to get attention. Yet I received a cable that same evening to say that it was just what she wanted.

Victor and I were distressed that Jacqueline Onassis was so often the target of criticism. Throughout our relationship she was extremely courteous and competent: indeed the courtesy was positively embarrassing. On the morning after our meeting, a messenger from the Ritz appeared in the pandemonium of our house-moving, bringing a letter saying how much she had enjoyed meeting us. A few days later another letter arrived at the new flat with much the same message, and only then did I realise that the hostess had twice thanked her guests without the guests thanking their hostess!

The book, called *In the Russian Style*, was really a companion to the exhibition rather than a catalogue. It was sold in paperback at the Met, and afterwards it was published in hardback in America, and in Britain by Thames and Hudson. It was amusing to hear Misha relate the shock-effect that the Met director and Mrs Onassis had had on the staff of the Soviet museums from which costumes were chosen, many of whom were his acquaintances. Those in positions of authority in the Soviet system were accustomed to lay down the law unchallenged. In this case they found themselves up against an extremely determined couple who knew what they wanted and meant to get it. They turned down items which the museums had picked for them, making it clear that this was their exhibition and the choice was to be theirs also. By all accounts it was a great success.

12

Genius comes in many shapes and sizes. My father's genius was on a small scale but it was the real thing: he had a genius for friendship. He loved poetry and art, and he loved those who created them. He wrote to them about their work, and his sympathetic appreciation was received not only with joy but respect. They in turn wrote to him; he kept their letters; and my sister and I gave some 1,500 of them to the Library of Somerville. (We gave them, too, William Rothenstein's portrait and Max Beerbohm's caricature of our father; Paul Nash's landscape drawings and portrait of me, made at our Oxfordshire home; and our father's remarkable album, where friends wrote poems and made drawings, to which I shall return later.) I have combed those letters to choose extracts that illuminate my father's relationship with the writers; which bring out their feelings about their work and that of others; and which give a flavour of the period, covering two world wars. (Because some of the names will be unfamiliar today, a brief Who's Who is given at the end of the book.)

Almost universally, correspondence that began 'Dear Dr Withers' would soon change to 'Dear – or even 'Dearest' – Percy'. Conventional endings would become expressions of deep affection. They all wrote of their happy visits to my parents' Oxfordshire homes. Those homes were charming, my mother's housekeeping skills ensured comfort, and harassed lives enjoyed a break. But it was primarily for my father that they went, and when they were not with him they welcomed his letters – and replied to them, even if only to keep the correspondence going. It is true that my father had plenty of time on his hands and took a delight in letter-writing; but in using those things to create and maintain close friendships – friendships with gifted men, absorbed in creative (and much-resented uncreative) work – I think he showed a quality that could be called genius.

Noticeable in the letters is the writers' gratitude at my father's appreciation of their work. Wilfrid Gibson wrote: 'I feel that if it were not that writing is its own great reward such letters as yours would be recompense for years of penal servitude.' F.L. Griggs, a distinguished artist, wrote: 'Your most kind praise of my work, and obviously very real affection for it, touches me deeply, and encourages me more than I could tell you.' From Robin Flower came: 'Your letter gave me the greatest pleasure. That you should rate the poems so highly is a great reassurance to me, who am rather diffident about my work.' Gordon Craig, after sending a package of his etchings from Italy, wrote: 'I'm very glad you like these things of mine. It's so rare an experience for me to hear an expression of the kind that I begin to think it has gone to my head – and that accounts for my crying out to my son, "Here's someone who likes my work!! Quick, send him all I've done to look at!"' Such letters reaffirm the creative power of praise.

My father's letters were looked forward to and enjoyed for themselves. John Freeman wrote: 'The most generous of correspondents has fallen away, the most punctual become erratic, the stars no longer keep their courses or the sun his eastern appointment. The postman never comes here and the letter box hangs rusty on its hinges.' The artist Ethel Walker wrote: 'You are an outstanding genius as a writer. How much I have enjoyed your letters! I am so touched by your appreciation of the watercolour.' My father had bought her watercolour *Lazarus*. He loved it, and hung it over the mantelpiece in his library. My sister chose it from his pictures, after his death, and left it to the Friends Meeting House in Saffron Walden.

Even A.E. Housman – not one to be lavish with praise – wrote: 'It is true that I do not write to you, but then there are few people to whom I do, and never willingly. You write with ease, elegance and evident enjoyment, whereas I hate it. Like Miss

Squeers, I am screaming out loud all the time I write, which takes off my attention rather and I hope will excuse mistakes.' In spite of that, Housman wrote sixty-five letters to my father. Most touching is one he wrote shortly before his death: 'I am sorry to have written tartly: my intention was not so; and indeed the extreme and undeserved kindness and generosity of your letter moved me almost to tears.' I think Robert Bridges's wife put her finger on it in a letter to my mother: 'I always enjoy what Percy writes: is it partly because he is not afraid of expressing his kindly feelings, as some are? and so I feel cheered and encouraged.'

As their poetry brought in little of the money needed, writers supplemented it with reviewing and lecturing and poetry readings (for publicity, if not for pay), and they poured out their frustrations to my father. Walter de la Mare, before recognition came to him, wrote: 'Wretched lectures stare me in the face and refuse to look away.' Wilfrid Gibson wrote of a poetry-reading tour to ten cities, and added bitterly: 'I wouldn't go if the going did not bring in a few very necessary guineas. Poetry and poverty certainly lead to desperate devices to make a living.' Artists, too, suffered from pot-boiling work which kept them from their true vocation. F.L. Griggs had to supplement his income by illustrating 'Highways and Byways' books. Before setting out for Leicestershire he wrote: 'I'm away on my loathed and lonely tour.' He, with another leading etcher, brought back into circulation several of Samuel Palmer's etchings, by making, with devoted care, a small number of prints from newly discovered plates.

Lascelles Abercrombie, a man of enormous vitality, with a passionate interest in every facet of life, was a reluctant, though inspiring, lecturer, and despised himself as such, writing: 'I have several lumps of old lecture-stuff which might work up into book form, but the labour of re-hashing these old gobbets is inexpressibly repugnant to me.' And: 'Of my Merton job – of course it's a great honour; but it accentuates the odiousness of the odious business I must pursue, loathing myself for a humbug, and despising myself for having failed in all my ambitions large and small.'

In the first days of the 1914–18 war Lascelles wrote: 'I am immensely busy with lectures at the Stratford Conference –

foolery in days like these! But probably my last chance of earning money for months, if not years.' My father had raised money for memorial tablets to George Gissing and Francis Thompson at Owens College, Manchester. Now he wrote to the Prime Minister, Mr Asquith, applying for a pension from the Civil List for Lascelles; and it was granted on condition that my father acted as trustee. Later, when Lascelles became professor of poetry at Liverpool, and no longer needed the pension, he wrote my father a letter that ranks among the finest I know:

> Now it is brought to an end, let me just say this: that never did any man have truer or lovelier friendship than yours, and never was any man more aware of it than I am. A debt in this life still owing, still to pay, is mine: only to be cancelled in that world where all things cancel out, and action becomes one with reaction, debt with payment, and every opposite unites: a world of which I sometimes think I have glimpses.

One marvellous piece of financial good fortune came to three poets – Walter de la Mare, Lascelles Abercrombie and Wilfrid Gibson. Their friend, Rupert Brooke, who died early in the war, had made a will leaving all the royalties from the sale of his poetry to be divided between them. Neither he nor they had any conception what that would mean. For years to come edition after edition would be published, in response to an unprecedented demand.

When Lascelles died, *English* (the magazine of the English Association) published 'The Homage of Friends', to which my father contributed, saying: 'If ever man warmed both hands before the fire of life, it was he; and with both hands again he imparted the warmth. Where the most of mankind enjoy, he exulted.' Gordon Bottomley wrote: 'He was one of those great lonely souls like Mantegna, whose grip on power has something fierce and sharp in it, with the weight and edge of granite. The best apples are the hardest at first; they do not yield suddenly even to the sun – but they keep the longest.' Oliver Elton wrote, several years after Lascelles's death: 'I too have been not only regretful but startled at the "neglect" into which his muse has fallen (for the time being). I think he will always have a limited but secure public. Think how Donne, and now Christopher Smart, had to wait decades for recognition.'

The work of creative artists is apt to fall out of favour in the period following their deaths, but I think it is foolish to ignore, and even ridicule, the opinions of their contemporaries because one is then, by implication, invalidating judgements now being made on the writers and artists of one's own time. Reviewers of a recent book on Robert Bridges have almost gloated over the fact that he is no longer read, or even known, yet it was not for nothing that John Freeman wrote about his *New Verse* (1925): 'I don't care how little or how much of philosophy there is in it, for there's sure to be so much of Bridges in it, and I admire him with the feeling one usually reserves for great and noble things of the past.'

Robert Bridges, then Poet Laureate, used to come for the day from Oxford to Souldern, with his wife. He was a splendid-looking man, with such health that, in his eighties, he cracked walnuts with his teeth and his grey hair was thick and springy. My father took good, informal photographs of his visitors and his snapshot of Bridges, in a deckchair in our garden, was used as the frontispiece of his *New Verse*, the sitter himself writing: 'I think there is no doubt that the pictures are the "best" portraits that have been done of me. Certainly they seem to please my family and my friends.'

John Freeman was unusual in the way he made his living, with a City insurance firm. 'I'm not generally my own master, any more than Charles Lamb was. I work in an office blessedly unrelated to letters, and so live a double life of a kind which has come, after so many years, to suit me. I do wonder whether in my case of oppressive necessity it is not better to have something secure and an easy mind than something uncertain and a troubled mind.' It amused him to write: '*The Caliphs*, which you were about the first to welcome, is being read to various gatherings in England and Paris by Edith Sitwell, who can't write often enough to praise it!' About his own work he wrote:

I'm busy, but don't pity me because I like work, even if it is prose. I love writing prose as I love watching a river; and prose is a river, holding the shadows of trees and clouds and the harsher line of the banks, with a snake wriggling up and lifting his head above the water until I move. Inspiration is that snake, and I have but to leave it alone and when it has gone, to remember the furrow of its swimming and the bands of its back.

And again: 'This queer world – it perpetually amuses and astonishes – bores never.'

Another 'part-time' poet was Robin Flower, who had a senior post in the department of manuscripts at the British Museum. In 1938 he wrote:

I had a curious experience today. Hodgsons are selling Thomas Hardy's books and had a private view. It was an interesting show; all the books presented to him by authors, with the usual inscriptions, and a few letters. This kind of break-up of a man's collections always saddens me, and I said as much to Sidney Cockerill. 'Not a bit,' says Sidney. 'I like seeing them going about the world.' The world! These things, to him, are the natural prey of museums and collectors. But I have never been able to reconcile myself to that view. I can only see the last curtain going down on a man's life, all the friendships and intimate relationships flying apart in a horrible saleroom, with the dealers putting a price on them.

Robin Flower was passionately Irish, and translated Gaelic poetry. His special affection was for the Blasket Islands, lying off the Irish coast, out in the Atlantic Ocean. Years later, fresh light was thrown on the Blaskets, for me, by a member of the Irish Civil Service, whose rare visits were greeted with appropriate hospitality. 'When,' he recalled, 'at around two in the morning they opened a fresh barrel of beer, I could tell that they meant to make an evening of it.' In my early days in London I was invited for an eye-opening weekend with the Flowers. I had imagined writers shutting themselves away, with the closed door giving a 'Do not disturb' message; but though the door of Robin's study was shut, he was not inside it. He could do creative writing only when out in the sitting-room, with his children wrestling on the floor across his feet, and coming on top of him, head first, over the back of the sofa. He and I both had to catch a train to London on Monday morning, but there was no time for breakfast. We ran to the station, taking bites of Mrs Flower's marmalade sandwiches when we paused for breath.

Alice Meynell was the only woman among my father's poet friends: indeed, I believe, the only recognized woman poet of her time. My father first got to know her and her husband by correspondence when fund-raising for a memorial tablet to Francis Thompson, whom the Meynells had befriended with great generosity. Wilfred Meynell wrote that some mutual acquaintance 'gives me a fine account of you. You are, he says, among men what a greyhound is among dogs'. The Meynells had gifted children – chief among them, Francis, founder of the incomparable Nonesuch Press. In her last letter to my father she wrote: 'My dear friend, I will not quarrel with him who told you that I was more unwell (though I am not) because the mistake brought me another sign of your kindness for me, in your letter. With thanks from my heart, dear friend, I am ever your affectionate A.M.' But she was much 'more unwell', and it was her husband who wrote on her behalf, 'I am still in office as Secretary, and I write to give you her thanks for your letter and her acceptance of that most delectable of tips – a dedication' (of the second of my father's Lake District books, *Friends in Solitude*). She died before it came out in 1923, and the dedication read: 'Affectionately and reverently, to the memory of Alice Meynell, in the fourteenth year of friendship.'

Publishers were often the subject of correspondence, and this set me thinking that our entire knowledge of the writing of our own day (and of the past, if work has gone out of print) comes to us through firms whose criterion is bound to be its estimated sales. And their judgement is not always sound. A.E. Housman told my father that *A Shropshire Lad* had been turned down by four publishers before it was accepted, after which it has remained in print for almost a century. How much talented work, by less persistent writers, must have gone unpublished! The commercial aspect of the theatre is emphasized by Edward Gordon Craig, quoted later; and the same applies to all the arts. A painter gets a show only if a gallery thinks his work will sell; a composer's music is played if it is likely to attract an audience; and when books, plays, paintings and music are presented to the public, their success still depends heavily on reviews – which are not always dependable.

The name of Walter de la Mare will be one of the most familiar today. He had a charming personality, and an endearing way of making people feel that they had something important to divulge, especially in matters of the occult – an absorbing subject of his poetry and prose. He wrote to my father in 1921 regretting that he had not 'introduced you long long ago to Miss M. She is a little tired, poor dear, and may take a dip in that delicious pool before she scrambles up the stone steps and taps on the door. I know you will be gentle'. This was his novel *Memoirs of a Midget* (1922), about which Wilfrid Gibson wrote: 'I have been reading de la Mare's "Midget" with the keenest satisfaction. The reviewers gave it perfunctory praise, but none of them seem to have realised the uniqueness of the achievement. It is indeed a "world in a grain of sand".' He added: 'You must have had great times with de la Mare and Lascelles together. Two keen minds with very far from "but a single thought"!'

After a serious illness de la Mare wrote: 'The machinery is getting a little less rusty, but a few cogs are still missing. Jinnie reminded me of what seemed a perfectly withering remark which I had made when I was pretty bad. Poor soul, she had to retire behind my bed in case the tears should come. She asked, would I like any flowers or fruit? My reply was that it was too late for fruit and too early for flowers!' Much later he wrote:

I, too, grow old, and the moment one is under the weather the fact of age looms into view like a shark out of the sea. As for 'time's winged chariot', its rumble is perpetually in my ears, too; and it's curious how unexpectedly one finds oneself looking forward so small a distance and looking back so long. Positive novelties in life are very rare. I never even faintly realised what a pacifying experience it is to become a grandfather. It is a sort of coming into port.

Gordon Bottomley became a frequent visitor and prolific correspondent. He was a large man, with the curious combination of dark hair and red beard. When very young he had developed a tubercular lung, the killer-disease of that period. Not unnaturally he had been scared into a semi-invalid state, and suffered symptoms which often sent him home in alarm. He was entranced with Scotland, and absorbed its history and its myths. A sequel to the novel or play of an earlier author has quite often been written, but Gordon wrote a play about the girlhood of Lady Macbeth. It was called *Gruach*, and I found it fascinating. I was still at school, it was the turn of our house to present a play, and I asked Gordon if we might do it. He was delighted. My part was that of a clairvoyant servant, who acted out, in a trance, the murderous future of her young mistress. It went down well with the school, and later was played in the theatres of several Scottish cities.

One thing of inestimable value Gordon Bottomley did for us: he persuaded my parents to buy a gramophone, and gave them a list of suggested records: Bach, Beethoven, Mozart, Wagner, Byrd and Boccherini. We had always lived miles from any town, let alone a town with a concert hall. Music didn't exist for us till we had that gramophone, and then we played it almost every night: an addition to my father's regular reading aloud of poetry.

Staying with Sturge Moore, Gordon wrote: 'In a few moments a dear old woman will enter my bedroom with two brass hot-water jugs and a benevolent smile, and I shall remember that Tennyson was her particular crony, and that she nursed Carlyle through his last illness.' This leads me to a story told to my father by a lunch guest at the Tennysons'. It was the first time she had met the great man, and she was eager to hear great words; but the only remark he made throughout the meal concerned a plate of meat carved by his son: 'How often have I told you, Hallam – beef thin, mutton thick.'

He also wrote of 'an evening with the Binyons. How I love

that Museum house, the gracious melancholy of its architecture and the sweetness of its inhabitants'. I, too, visited Laurence Binyon and his wife, in one of the wings of the British Museum where department heads then lived; and I heard him express the sense of insignificance that came over him as, four times a day, he crossed the grilled passageways that yawned above and below, to reveal the vast stockrooms of the Library.

Gordon's interest in historic houses – and his awareness that my father was on the Council of the National Trust – brought a letter drawing attention to East Riddlesden Hall, near Keighley, 'the most notable piece of man-made beauty that time has left there. The Tudor and Jacobean halls and manor-houses of West Yorkshire once rivalled Cotswold houses in number and architectural interest; but the Industrial Revolution wiped them half out. In this case, the speculator threatens to destroy the Hall for the sake of its material'. It is now safely listed in the National Trust's annual publication – one of over 1,300 historic properties open to the public through their good offices.

In January 1939 Gordon wrote:

I wonder if your thoughts keep returning day in and day out, as mine do, to the idea, threading through everything else, 'Yeats is dead – Yeats is dead.' Ever since I became conscious of great poetry, he has been There; the source of such supreme delights that even his vanity and his excessive but not unjustified pride never seemed to matter in the light of what he was doing and could do. 'And these things come not again.' One realises how much of one's life has been lived – how much impoverished the rest of it is bound to be. And all this so soon after Lascelles' going, who also was a beacon and a portent in my skies.

Poetry recitals were very much part of the literary scene between the wars. My father's friends frequently read poems at the Oxford Festival of Spoken Poetry – an annual event organized by John Masefield, after one of which Housman reported: 'I understand that Laurence [Binyon] did not read me very well, dropping his voice too much at impressive points.' Wilfrid Gibson described one at the Aeolian Hall in London, which 'could have been filled three times over if all the applications for tickets had been satisfied. The performance as a whole wasn't bad. Bottomley, Masefield, V. Sackville-West, the Sitwells and, I gather, Gibson, got their stuff across. Eliot, too, perhaps, though I am not sure of that. I managed to penetrate his reserve to some degree, and was interested to find him as baffled by the work of the younger poets as I am!'

There was one wild card in the pack of my father's friends. The others wrote and talked to him about one another; but this one was considered to be such an unlikely friend that they never stopped expressing their astonishment. It was A.E. Housman. His slim volume of poetry, *A Shropshire Lad*, was published in 1896. Not until 1922 did another volume appear: *Last Poems*. His whole reputation as a poet rested on those two books – yet that reputation was secure. As Gordon Bottomley wrote: 'Whether A.E.H. likes it or not, posterity will hear of him as a lyrical poet. He goes on writing beautiful poetry but is ashamed to own it.'

What Housman regarded as his real work was at Trinity College, Cambridge, where he was professor of Latin, and regarded as the outstanding classical scholar of his age. He appeared to enjoy an aloof reputation, so to attempt friendship was considered as unwise as to pat an unfriendly dog. On a snapshot my father took of him he commented: 'The photograph is not quite true to my own notion of my gentleness and sweetness of nature, but neither perhaps is my external appearance.' But my father was not easily put off; and although they could hardly have been more different in temperament, a correspondence began, annual visits took place, and a friendship was formed that lasted until Housman's death. Few would have had letters saying, 'At any date in July I shall be free and joyful to come and stay for a day or two'; and, 'I rejoice at the prospect of seeing you this term.' Lascelles Abercrombie, writing to my mother, spoke of 'the affectionate kindness of which you and Percy have the secret, and in which one lives at Souldern as in an element. Well can I understand how it is that that shy unicorn A.E. Housman will visit none but you!'

Years after Housman died Richard Aldington threw light on his character in a lecture at University College, London, where Aldington had been a student when Housman was a professor there. He said: 'Housman would walk past us as if he were enclosed in an invisible envelope of frigidity, which repelled not only any familiarity but the slightest human contact. The real reason for his extraordinary behaviour was that he was hopelessly and helplessly shy and sensitive, as well as proud and exacting.' Aldington then read a passage from T.E. Lawrence's *Seven Pillars of Wisdom*. 'There was my craving to be liked – so strong and nervous that never could I open myself friendly to another. There was a craving to be famous, and contempt for my passion for distinction made me refuse every offered honour.' Against that passage Housman wrote 'This is me', and he himself refused the highest honorary degrees from many universities, and all other honours – even the Order of Merit.

It was intriguing that he himself eventually made a spyhole in the wall of reserve he had built round himself, by his famous lecture, 'The Name and Nature of Poetry', in which he said: 'Poetry indeed seems to me more physical than intellectual.' Having been asked to define poetry, he said: 'I could no more define poetry than a terrier can define a rat, but both recognize the object by the symptoms which it provokes.' And he went on to quote from the Book of Job: 'A spirit passed before my face; the hair of my flesh stood up.' Of another symptom he said: 'I can only describe it by borrowing a phrase from one of Keats' last letters, where he says, speaking of Fanny Brawne, "Everything that reminds me of her goes through me like a spear".' He added: 'The seat of this sensation is the pit of the stomach.'

It was Grant Richards (Housman's publisher and my father's) who introduced them, when war-work took my parents to Cambridge for the last years of the 1914–18 war. William Rothenstein knew them both, too, and wrote: 'I am glad you have been seeing him. I have a great admiration for him, both as a poet and as a man. His opinions are less expected than those of anyone I know, and there is a finish and hardness about him which delights me.'

Soon after the war, when my parents had settled at Souldern,

Housman came to stay with them. He and my father shared two interests outside literary ones: church architecture and weather records. These last were a real passion with my father. He had a registered rain-gauge, placed at a minimum distance from any tree or building. He measured the rainfall every day, and sent in the record monthly; and every day, too, he made notes on the weather, the temperature and flowering dates. So he recognized a kindred spirit in Housman, whose letter dated 23 April 1928 read: 'This is not a late spring; but there have been so many early springs that people have forgotten the proper times for leaves and flowers to come out. For 20 years or so, from 1887 onward, I noted these things in a diary, on the strength of which I inform you that the lilac usually comes into bloom on May 7; and it is opening now by Magdalene Bridge, though I admit that it is always early there.'

There is a sparse dryness in Housman's letters that is entirely characteristic. His Trinity College news was: 'Death and marriage are raging through this College with such fury that I ought to be grateful for having escaped both.' And in one Boxing Day letter he recounted:

Rutherford's daughter, married to another Fellow of Trinity, died suddenly a day or two ago; the wife of the Emeritus Professor of Greek, who himself is paralysed, has cut her throat with a razor which she had bought to give her son-in-law; I have a brother and a brother-in-law both seriously ill and liable to drop dead any moment; in short, Providence has given itself up to the festivities of the season. A more cheerful piece of news is that I have just published the last book I shall ever write, and that I now mean to do nothing for ever and ever. It is one of my more serious works, so you will not read it.

The New Year's Eve banquet at Trinity was an important event for Housman. One year he wrote: 'I will remember you at midnight, when I shall be drinking to absent friends in stout and oysters, which are very salubrious and which I take medicinally to neutralise the excesses of Christmas. When you give

Mrs Winslow's soothing syrup to a baby, "the little darling wakes up as bright as a button": and so do I on New Year's Day.' Housman had a much-revered predecessor in the seventeenth/eighteenth-century scholar, Richard Porson, famous also as a lover of wine. There is a story that at one of Trinity's celebration dinners, when speeches were being made after much eating and drinking, Housman rose to his feet and spoke: 'This hall has seen many strange sights. It has seen Wordsworth drunk; it has seen Porson sober. Here stand I – a better scholar than Wordsworth and a better poet than Porson – betwixt and between.'

It was clear that, as a letter-writer, Housman suffered reproaches from my father, for he wrote: 'You are the most acrimonious of my correspondents, and insist on making a grievance of what you ought to regard as a natural phenomenon, like the voice of the peacock or the smell of the goat.' But he could throw an unexpected gift into a letter, as when he wrote during a papal election:

> It is a fearful thing to be
> The Pope.
> That cross will not be laid on me
> I hope.
> A righteous God would not permit
> It.
> The Pope himself must often say
> After the labours of the day
> 'It is a fearful thing to be
> Me.'

After my parents moved from Souldern to Epwell, Housman wrote: 'I am glad to hear that you have secured a spot which in some respects at any rate is so much to your taste. I regret to observe that my convenience has not been your prime consideration and that I shall have a much longer journey between me and your Domain.' Surprisingly, he had noticed the part my parents played in the life of Souldern, and added: 'I don't know what the village will do without you.' But his health was beginning to fail, and he wrote of a tour in Alsace-Lorraine: 'I suppose it did me some good; but improvement is infinitesmal. My life is bearable, but I do not want it to continue, and I wish it had ended a year and a half ago. The greatest blessing and the one undiluted bounty of this life is a sudden and painless end.'

Housman died in 1936, and my father's friends sent their condolences and their appreciation of his close friendship. Lascelles wrote:

Now that the end has come it is a dreadful shock. A great scholar – one had only to look at his work to see that; a great poet; and whatever may be said, a great man. It is a loss such as the death of Bridges or Hardy; and we shall not know such a loss again. I know what a grief to you his death must be, for you and he were bound by an affection which I believe he gave to no one else.

G.M. Young, referring to my father's article in the *New Statesman*, said:

It brought up a keen regret that I had not met him with you, and now am never to meet him. I was glad that you did not shrink from the discordant note. There was something in his writing, and no doubt in his personality, that reminded me of the scream at the end of a blackbird's song. One expected it, one got used to it, but wished it wasn't there. You must have written from a full heart as well as a full memory, and there must be other things to say which probably only you know.

G.M. Trevelyan wrote: 'Thank you very much indeed for your most kind letter which I greatly appreciated. It was like you, with your warm heart, to write it and to tell me that the greatest of Trinity men of this 20th century, Housman, said he would approve of me as Master. That is indeed an honour. You are the best living evidence on what he was and thought.'

It was observations such as these that encouraged my father to write the story of their friendship, and the light it had thrown on Housman's personality. It was published in 1940 by Jonathan

Cape under the expressive title *A Buried Life*. My father didn't gloss over the difficulties of the relationship when experienced at close quarters: the taciturnity, the flashes of anger, the times when appreciation was expected yet not forthcoming. Housman's extreme contrasts of mood are described by my father during the only occasion when I was present. I had blown in from London and, 'showing complete freedom from self-consciousness and awe', had sparked off a lively exchange throughout the evening. The next morning – his last – 'he was glum and tongue-tied. He gave a curt good-bye to my wife and daughter. At the waiting car he made not the smallest reference to the visit, repeated the same bare, almost impersonal good-bye, but as he grasped my hand, wordlessly, he turned on me the saddest and most haunting countenance I had ever seen on any face'.

My father felt the need to write; his letter-writing was a time-filling substitute for the writing of books. His first had been *Egypt of Yesterday and Today*, a commission carried out during an Egyptian visit and illustrated with his own photographs. He had been commissioned to compile an anthology of poetry and prose from the sixteenth to the twentieth century, *Garland of Childhood*, which must have entailed an immense amount of reading. *In a Cumberland Dale*, and its sequel, *Friends in Solitude*, were imaginative re-creations of life in his best-loved region. He idolized Wordsworth, and as he read widely about him and his circle he became fascinated by Wordsworth's sister Dorothy – a powerful presence about whom little was known, apart from her *Journals*. He must have talked to friends about his interest in her because Robin Flower wrote that he had been reading the *Journals*: 'What an eye she had! She can put an impression down in a flying touch that gives you the very moment isolated from the restlessness of time.' My father felt that new material was needed – and this was in the possession of Gordon Wordsworth, a descendant. His first approach met with a cordial response; but then came a blank refusal – perhaps in anticipation of more of the 'revelations' about which John Freeman wrote: 'I'm vexed that Gordon Wordsworth should interpose his own indifference to prevent your eagerness. The Wordsworth revelations of the last years make me suspect that we don't know half.' He was referring to the 'revelation' that, as a young man, Wordsworth had had an affair in France, from which a child was born.

In his disappointment my father cast around for another subject, and considered writing his reminiscences. He saw this as a kind of extension of his book on Housman, to cover the whole circle of his friends. He confided his plan to Hugh Fausset, whom we first knew as a King's College choir scholar. Fausset had become a literary biographer and reviewer, and he responded warmly: 'There can be few men living who have associated on such terms of intimacy as you have with some of the rarer spirits of your time. I can imagine no one with a collection of letters like yours.' Lascelles Abercrombie added encouragement: 'Few people can have been so rich in friendship as you. Such a book as you describe would be a picture of the time, and of the choicest spirits of the time.' However, nothing came of it. I think his precarious health made my father unable to tackle a project that meant sifting through a mountain of material. I have quoted here from only a fraction of the letters in the Somerville Library.

Among my father's artist friends the one most closely associated with our family and our home was Paul Nash. In 1923 Paul wrote: 'Many thanks for your charming letter with its proposals. The whole conception makes a strong appeal to me. My wife is thrilled by the idea of a new hat. In fact we accept without reserve. I will make you the best drawing I possibly can.' The idea and the commission was that Paul and his wife should visit Souldern, and that my father would buy at least one of the drawings he made. In fact it was the beginning of a whole series of visits — sometimes spread over weeks — which resulted in paintings, watercolour drawings and woodcuts, of which my father bought six drawings and several woodcuts.

After that first visit Paul wrote: 'Everyone admires the Souldern scenes, but especially the drawing I shall call "The Hanging Garden".' This was the view from his bedroom, which looked out on the village pond, with a garden rising steeply up the hill behind. He made at least one painting, two drawings and a woodcut of this subject. Later, when the Souldern work was included in an exhibition, he wrote: 'I have been told by quite a few discerning ones that it's a complete advance, and some of the best paintings I have done. Souldern is always inspiration to me – as much for its mental atmosphere as for anything it offers of actual subject matter. I would like to have a long talk. May I run down in the Spring? I should love Souldern in the Spring.' It was characteristic that his favourite subjects were trees. In a letter to Gordon Bottomley he wrote: 'I have tried to paint trees as tho' they were human beings; because I sincerely love and worship trees and know they are people and wonderfully beautiful people.'

Paul's letters were often undated, so I can't be sure when he wrote the following:

I am getting considerably frightened by my fame – altho' I am happy if it seems to realize the hopes of my friends! But seriously, I am embarrassed. I have done so little. I want to do so much, and so much of my time gets wasted, life is so complicated, the years speed by. My latest commission is to paint from the window of Whistler's White House in Chelsea, which seems to have been disembowelled and Venetianised, and is now inhabited by a quaint old American lady whom I disconcerted by selecting the bathroom-cum-lavatory to make my picture from. I thought I heard a ghostly chuckle on the air.

Another undated letter read:

I should like you to have seen the new pictures to judge of my development. I feel it is there and continuing, but along new lines. A one-man show is always good for me. I learnt a lot from mine; weaknesses which one cannot see on the easel stare out when the painting is on the walls of a gallery. At first, when the pictures were stood around the room, I had a moment of despair; but after lunch, when they were hung up, I felt more satisfied with their looks; but, Lord, how glad I was when it was over! I got to feeling a kind of fraud; for you know it is not possible to think of one's work as having got anywhere.

Just as my father's poet friends deplored the time they were forced to spend on everything except writing poetry, Paul also complained,

In the old days I had leisure and I mean to have leisure again. Now I'm driven and it don't suit me. Now I'm a bit of a painter and a pedagogue and a lecturer and a designer for the theatre and for textiles. But it won't do. So I've quite firmly resigned my usher's job at the RCA and I'm not going to lecture again if I can possibly afford not to; and when my present jobs for books are cleared off I'm going to settle down to paint again.

He was as good as his word.

Paul Nash did a great deal more abstract thinking than most artists, and there was a definite philosophy behind much of his work. Magritte called him 'A Master of the Object' because he saw a profound significance in such things as the Avebury Stones and the huge carcasses of uprooted trees which inhabit his 'Monster Fields'. When in 1933 he and Henry Moore were founder members of Unit One, which set out the aims of a movement in English architecture, painting and sculpture, he wrote in its manifesto: 'We, today, must find new symbols to express our creative environment. In some cases this will take the form of an abstract art, in others we may look for some different nature of imaginative research.' He went on to describe a field near Avebury: 'Two rough monoliths, miraculously patterned with black and orange lichen. A mile away, a green pyramid casts its gigantic shadow. In the hedge, the white trumpet of a convolvulus turns from the spiral stem, following the sun. In my art I would solve such an equation.' He shared with William Blake a profound belief in the meaning of all creation. In 1795 Blake wrote: 'I see Everything I paint In This World, but Everybody does not see alike. The tree which moves some to tears of joy is in the Eyes of others only a Green thing which stands in the way. But in the Eyes of the Man of Imagination, Nature is Imagination itself. As a man is, so he sees.'

After my father had bought a drawing, Paul wrote:

It is always a pleasure for the artist to hear a spontaneous expression of enthusiasm for his work, but it really touches him when he realises that someone has been carried away to the extent of unlocking a hollow cash box, parting with the last note but one, and then reached for the purple ink and made a generous confession of his emotion. I am now concentrating on oils, and think I have made some advance in that medium. Many of the paintings are thicker – more solid-looking – and many of the new ones are of Still Life – which fascinates me. Nothing can be quite as absorbing, or so satisfying to paint.

Like many artists, Paul wrote well: so unfair, when writers are seldom able to draw. He contributed many articles to art magazines, and in 1938 he wrote about a book later published as *Outline*: 'I am in the midst of a book – a kind of autobiography, but concerned mainly with my encounters with places rather than with people – the effect places had upon me and I upon places – can you imagine that? – illustrated by drawings and paintings. I am enjoying writing it – so far.' He was also a skilful photographer, using a camera as a kind of sketchbook to recall some composition of landscape, and with close-ups to show details like the bark of a tree or the markings on a stone. Such reminders became more and more necessary as asthma made prolonged outdoor work impossible for him.

Again undated: 'The Redfern show seems to have been practically entirely a success! – just one of those flukes of chance. I had not had an exhibition for some years and I happened to give what people seemed able and willing to buy. Apart from that I was accorded quite an enthusiastic "Press". Altogether I felt a little bewildered and slightly suspicious.' He had previously written in all sincerity that an artist must be ready to resist the favours and expectations of the public, making the acute observation: 'One and all of us are invited to please. We are sure to please if we go back or stand still.' This he was determined not to do.

Paul suffered increasingly from asthma. He wrote: 'I am infinitely better since I got my German inhaler; in fact, if I hadn't found it, I don't know what sort of state I should be in by now. It has simply given me life, and I hope will prove definitely curative in the long run. But you know what asthma is; few diseases are more subtle, more elusive.'

The inhaler was not 'definitely curative'. In the summer of 1941 Paul wrote: 'Before the world comes to an end, or at least so much of it that matters to you and me, I should like to feel we are reunited after an inexplicable blackout. You are not the only friend I have lost touch with: for explanation – I have moved about hardly at all for nearly a year. Before that I was tied to London with work and medical treatment. When one lives like that one becomes less and less mobile, one ceases to bother, one neglects one's friends.' My father must have reassured him, for he replied: 'I was so glad to have your warm genuine letter. It was a great relief to meet such a response.'

In spite of ill-health, Paul again became a war artist, as he had been in the 1914–18 war. He worked with the Air Ministry and the Ministry of Information but, this time, not going far afield but concentrating on aspects of air warfare as experienced at home. The best-known of those paintings is *Totes Meer*: the piled-up wreckage of German aircraft shot down over Britain. About this he wrote: 'There lived here in death innumerable vehicles of destruction all directed by human agency, some in the manner of ships manned by crews, others as closely bound up with man as a horse with its rider.' We have reason to be proud of the war artists of both wars. Not only were they the outstanding figures of their time but they were imaginatively handled – in the last war by Sir Kenneth Clark, who assigned each artist to the area best suited to him: Henry Moore to the night population of the London Underground; Graham Sutherland to the destruction and fires of the air raids; Paul Nash to the monstrous graveyard of bombers, and many others. Such creative work has a more permanent place in history than the actuality of photographs, and it makes an impressive show at the Imperial War Museum in London.

When the end of the war was in sight Paul wrote:

I spend about 60% of my energy on coughing and spitting, and a great many hours inhaling. My work suffers, of course; is slowed down; but Tooth's have wonderfully long-suffering people who have been waiting to buy my work. All the money I can keep goes towards a wonderful dream . . . the end of the War and escape from England – escape on to a ship to get to sea and some day to set foot on North Africa and find somewhere to live not far from the Desert, where the Atlas mountains stand against the far sky.

It is strange that an artist whose work is as closely identified with the English landscape as Constable's should have yearned for North Africa. I saw nothing of Paul during the war, when he lived in Oxford; and I missed a visit to Epwell, which produced several drawings. Two of these, acquired by the present owner, hang in the house from which they were made. All I can think is that, worn out by asthma, he longed for a kinder climate. His dream was never realized. He died in 1946.

My father had a very different relationship, in the twenties, with a very different artist, Edward Gordon Craig. They never met, for Craig lived permanently in Italy; but they exchanged many letters, and Gordon Craig seemed to take pleasure in sending over whole portfolios of his woodcuts – even though only about half a dozen were bought. He wrote: 'No matter whether you purchase any – just look at them, and send them back after a while. You are not to feel in the least embarrassed, or I shall then indeed begin to be seriously vexed with myself.'

Craig was the son of Ellen Terry, and had first appeared on the London stage in 1889, under the direction of Henry Irving. He went on to become a brilliant theatrical designer. I am not clear what went wrong; but he had abandoned England and settled in Italy, where he founded a school in Florence for The Art of the Theatre, and devoted himself to making woodcuts. These were mainly figure subjects – characters out of Shakespeare or the Bible, or out of his head. His letters were wonderfully flamboyant, in appearance and in substance, but so incoherent that they are hard to quote from. Constant bitter references to theatrical subjects make one feel that that was where he really belonged. For instance:

I am glad you liked looking at the black things I sent you, but sorry to hear you are laid up in a London nursing home. I ought to be – but may just skip that and land tiptoe in a grave instead – unless they hurry up and offer me Drury Lane or Covent Garden, both of which playhouses are going to the dogs. But I hardly think this will occur to them in London – 'The Dancers' [presumably the Russian Ballet] appearing to them to be greater any day than 'Much Ado about Nothing' or 'Il Barbiere de Seviglia'.

When he lived in Rapallo Craig of course knew his neighbour, Max Beerbohm, who had made a caricature of my father when they met during the war. He wrote: 'I had a charming talk with Max about you and your "portrait" – the sketch I want you to have.' (Gordon Craig had asked Max to draw his recollection of my father which, quite naturally, years after their meeting, bore no resemblance to him.) He went on:

Max is so human when he is not divine or infernal, and in that he is all 3 in good measure. This humanity sits charmingly on him. He wonders . . . would his sketch hurt you . . . no, he thought best not give it to you . . . and then suddenly quietly came out his confession that sometimes when he had drawn someone . . . and drawn it all so nice and charming, the said person would say, 'Oh' and look 'Ah' and so on, and feel mortally wounded . . . and so he did more and more dread to touch paper with pencil. I shall send you the sketch and you are positively to like it or I shall be grieved. 'A handsome fine fellow with much charm and grace'; that's how he talks as he sketches you in.

Returning to theatrical subjects he wrote:

They are all saying that it is incredible that I've had no theatre in London for 20 years – yet when I asked for one – and I asked a dozen times – no one was found to give me an answer – much less a theatre. And, as usual, I did not want it so as to coin gold with – but so as to give out anything that

193

may be in me to the English people. The theatre has always been rather too commercially minded in England. Even Bernard Shaw, Barrie, Pinero and other play writers have become sticklers for big terms. The actors are hopelessly commercial. Casson and Miss Thorndike, so often looked on as being idealists, are typically commercial. Sir G Du Maurier, supposed to be one of the leaders of the Profession, is one of the followers of the commercial group. The facts are simple – they will only give a theatre to some one who will guarantee to run it on commercial lines – ie swindling lines. Really London is imbecile.

This bitter diatribe is almost his last letter. I know of no reason why the correspondence ended so abruptly.

In late Victorian and Edwardian times it was quite usual for people to have an album in which friends were asked to write their thoughts. A bindery had been set up in Broadway under the famous name of Katherine Adams, and my father commissioned a handsome leather-bound album from it, in which he intended to ask his friends to write their poems. Wilfrid Gibson, John Drinkwater and Lascelles Abercrombie made their contributions; then war broke out, my father taking charge of the convalescent home in Gloucestershire, and from there he made the acquaintance of William Rothenstein and Max Beerbohm, mentioned in Chapter 1. Soon those first entries in the album were followed by a Rothenstein drawing of Beerbohm and himself, captioned 'Max on his (almost) native heath'. Then came a Beerbohm caricature of Swinburne, 'from pre-natal memory', and verses in which he plays on the names of the earlier contributors.

Just as a play by Aeschylus or Ibsen
Doesn't inspire one to compose charades,
So am I loth to follow Mr Gibson
With one of my ignoble pasquinades.

Pierian rills and rivulets from which
Such men as Mr Drinkwater drink water
Aren't for the likes of me; I share a ditch
With Mr Sims and Mr Clement Shorter.

In fact, I know my place. Shall I yet shame
The vicinage of Lascelles Abercrombie
With prose as tawdry or with verse as tame
As that of poor iambic Master Dombey?

Though Burns has (doubtless) said 'All men are brithers'
Let me not spoil your lovely album, Withers!

13

I cannot end without riding some hobby-horses. They are unreliable mounts, which may fall at the first fence: but they are part of myself, and must be trotted out.

I support the demand for voluntary euthanasia. The arguments against it carry no weight with me, and are made by people with no experience of great age. We have all been adolescents, yet how many people, as parents, can relate to that strange mix of aggressive independence and insecurity when adolescence erupts in their own households? No one has ever been old except the old themselves – and so, I maintain, can any but the old conceive what it is like. The debate about voluntary euthanasia concentrates on the presence of a high degree of pain and the inevitability of imminent death. Of course what frightens us all is the prospect of long-drawn-out pain leading to death, rather than death itself. How often, when hearing that someone has dropped dead with a heart attack, do we think – how fortunate! What a wonderful way to go! But there are other things which haunt those who grow old; and I speak as a woman of eighty-eight.

We have been active; we dread immobility. We have been reasonably intelligent; we dread senility, with loss of memory and mental powers. We have been independent; we dread being utterly dependent, in an unloved second childhood, upon strangers. We have enjoyed saving money: intending it to bring security and pleasure to young people we love; we dread the prospect of our savings being eaten away by the costs of a 'home'.

Above all, we long to be remembered as the person we really are – not with that personality cruelly distorted by the onslaught of age, which may make us, at best, an object for pity and, at worst, for boredom and irritation. We simply want to banish all these fears by being able to say 'enough' when we have had enough; and have stated that wish years earlier, when in full health. Is our life not our own? At gatherings we have attended the time has come for us to say our farewells and leave, and someone has been kind enough to give us a lift. That is all we ask.

Fears are expressed that greedy relatives in charge of an old person will pressurize him or her to opt for euthanasia; but the safeguard, there, is that the option should be stated well in advance. Yet who would want to live, knowing of a death-wish in those nearest to them? I have one extra, personal reason for desiring the acceptance of voluntary euthanasia. Like my husband and my sister I have bequeathed my body for anatomical examination. Death from suicide requires an autopsy to determine the cause, and this renders one's body useless for examination. Voluntary euthanasia would enable doctors to give the cause of death in the usual way.

Such extraordinary arguments are used to attack voluntary euthanasia. God is invoked. How can these people assume that they know the mind of God? And why should they imagine that it pleases Him that life should be prolonged into a travesty of itself? And those who demand this are usually believers in an after-life, and ought to rejoice in the old gaining the blessings of heaven – or do they see them going to another place? Then the medical opposition trots out the Hippocratic oath. I do not want to undermine medicine's fine traditions (especially as my father was a doctor), but I find it absurd to treat as Holy Writ words uttered more than two thousand years ago. And Hippocrates was a doctor, not a deity. Probably he simply wished to state that doctors should dedicate themselves to the well-being of their patients: and is that condition met when human beings are kept alive in circumstances that would count as cruelty if applied to animals?

Throughout our lives, in a free society, we are encouraged to make our own decisions and do as we think best – provided our actions are not harmful to others. Who has given governments the right to thwart our wishes in this vital matter? Suicide is no longer a crime; but access to the means is always difficult and often impossible. What we need is professional help in a cause that would actually benefit society. The communities of the Western world will soon contain such a high proportion of elderly citizens that the working population will be unable to support them. Health services cannot cope with the ever-growing expectations of successful treatment for every disease that flesh is heir to – let alone with an ever-growing number living to an age when their conditions are incurable. Hospital wards are filled with such patients, while potentially active people suffer for lack of a bed. And families and friends suffer also. I knew two women: one well over eighty, in a wheelchair for eight years and longing to die; the other, much younger, who devoted her life to her friend's care. Twice the older woman was carried off to hospital, where the life she did not want was saved. The third time she died; and her exhausted friend died within six months. Who benefited from that misguided Health Service care?

The fact is that the word 'life' has been given an undeserved sanctity by those who oppose euthanasia and abortion. I do not think that any noun in our language possesses an absolute significance: the meaning is always modified by circumstance. 'Power' – to what end? 'Trust' – misplaced? 'Generosity' – wise or foolish? Even 'love' can be suspect. So 'pro-lifers' cannot be allowed to hijack their watchword and wave it as a banner proclaiming something absolute. They must be challenged by the reality that some lives are not worth living; that it would have been better for some people if they had never been born. 'Existence is not in itself a good thing. Our business here is not to live, but to live happily.' (A.E. Housman) It is incredible that our society should find a moral dilemma when a doctor hastens the death of an already dying patient, screaming with pain.

In the case of abortion, I believe it is for the woman to decide. There seems to me nothing more likely to lead to disaster, for everyone concerned, than an unwanted child. For the presence of a child changes the entire pattern of life – and it is only if that is acceptable, to say the least, that parent and child can hope for happiness. The appallingly abused children of whom charities like the NSPCC have knowledge, must surely be unwanted children whose parents resent their presence in the home: a presence which has caused agony to the child and criminal behaviour in the parents.

I think it is positively immoral to allow a child to live who is severely handicapped, physically or mentally. Parents who devote their lives to the care of a handicapped child (sometimes at the expense of their normal children) never seem to think that, when they grow old or die, that helpless, dependent creature will be shunted into some home, among strangers. Some civilizations have been more genuinely humane than ours. The Greeks exposed deformed infants.

Much of human behaviour arises from its level of expectation, and I think our Western civilization has come to expect too much. And it does not end there, for the spread of communication, world-wide, means that the people of countries which need decades of gradual development – and a development suited to their particular circumstances – are impatient to jump to a level that the West itself cannot sustain for all its members. In the Andes, the Indians are replacing their beautiful hand-made roof tiles with corrugated-iron sheeting and their handwoven ponchos with plastic capes, because these are 'modern'. A government official in the area told us that no roads were being built, for lack of cement. Victor and I had known an England where men with hammers broke up stones and steam-rollers crushed these into roads, so we suggested that the mountains could be quarried to that end. The official replied that the Indians would regard that as 'backward' and would take no part in it. Of course their economic situation desperately needs to be improved; but it is tragic that they should throw away their own civilization under the spell of a North American one which is unattainable, and also unsuitable.

Friends from countries where arranged marriages are universal have often said that the success of their system is proved by the relatively low number of marriage break-ups as compared with our 'love-matches'. But this is because their young people marry without such high – perhaps impossibly high – expectations of comradeship, sexual compatibility and faithfulness. I think our expectations have reached too high a level for our happiness. I do not mean to decry ambition, which is active, while expectation is passive: counting on getting what you want without doing much to bring it about. 'Il y a toujours un qui baise et un qui tourne la joue': not, surely, always, but quite often – and the passive partner should not be surprised if the active mate takes to kissing other cheeks. Disappointed expectation can take disruptive forms: in marriage, divorce; in the economic sphere, theft; and in both, violence.

Apart from possible nuclear disaster (from dangerous proliferation), I believe that two matters of overwhelming importance are now at the top of the world agenda. These are population and emigration, both of which have grown to such proportions as to be a threat to the physical and psychological well-being of the world. Just as a dwelling-place can be occupied in comfort only by a certain number of people (and when there are too many, quarrels break out), so the character of a place changes for the worse under the pressure of population growth. Even in Europe and the United States large numbers of citizens are unemployed, underfed, badly housed; but in other continents conditions are infinitely worse. Desperate people take desperate measures. In cities they turn to crime and prostitution; in the country they destroy their environment.

It is said that, once people are educated and prosperous, they will automatically have small families. Maybe; but how long will it take for the Third World population to become 'educated and prosperous'? One reads those terrible statistics: the lives of millions of children could be saved if they were given simple immunizing injections. But if they lived, would they die of hunger? Surely the urgent need is for a massive international effort to bring the practice of contraception to women worldwide. It is tragic that the poor of Latin America should be urged by their religion to be fruitful and multiply, thus swelling the hordes of homeless children who swarm in the city streets and – as a nuisance element, damaging to tourism – are murdered by police.

Highly developed countries have their problems too – admittedly minor, as compared with those of the Third World, but still seriously affecting that precious thing, the quality of life. One of my many privileges has been to be able to 'stand and stare', unhurried, alone or with one companion, at anything that caught my interest – at home or abroad, out of doors or in an art gallery or museum. Now, most travellers have to be part of a group, disgorged from a coach, harangued by a guide, shepherded about. I know that, if I had had to do my sightseeing in this way, my appreciation of what I saw would have been greatly diminished. I know because, on my last visit to St Petersburg, I was kindly invited to join a group when I (on a private visit) had no transport. In the halls where, thirty years ago, Victor and I had loitered (he, working with his camera while I made notes), our group now stood, wedged too tightly to take in any details, waiting for the group ahead to move on while the one behind was on our heels. It is, in itself, excellent that a great many people today want to see things that once interested only a few; but this welcome development raises problems. In the case of art galleries and museums it is impossible to appreciate the exhibits if one cannot have a leisurely, uninterrupted view. We ought therefore to be able to book a ticket for a limited number of viewers at a given hour, just as we do for a concert.

Now for that other problem, emigration. There was a period when Western countries – most notably the United States – could absorb emigrants successfully, making them welcome citizens who gave and received benefits to their own satisfaction and that of their host country. I think it has to be recognized that that time is past. All my life I have supported the cause of Human Rights. I was a founder member of Amnesty International, and regard it as the most important of all causes. I would want every genuine refugee to be offered a haven, but countries must put a limit on the entry of those who knock on their doors simply because it would suit them to come in.

The emigrant problem is not only one of numbers but of culture. Again, people sharing a house get along best if they come from much the same background. There could hardly be a stronger example of this than a small insurance company that

Victor used. Its head was a Scot, who had come south as a young man; yet he told Victor that every member of his staff was Scottish, saying, 'We feel more comfortable that way.' It is tragic that some multi-ethnic communities are falling apart, violently. We must try to ensure peaceful, satisfying lives for such communities; but it would be flying in the face of bitter experience to encourage their growth.

My ludicrously Utopian solution is for the United Nations to be made so rich and powerful that it could eventually help every country to achieve a government, and an economy, that would make its citizens content to stay at home. Even a tentative step in this direction would relieve the present pressure – under which the whole character of nations is changing, and emigrants are not getting the opportunities, or even the security, they looked for. If two parts of Germany cannot come together without resentment on one side and disappointment on the other, what hope is there for the integration of people who share nothing but a common humanity?

I am concerned at the emergence of all these isms: élitism, racism, sexism, which are causing people to suppress their speech – and, with it, their thinking – in order not to offend the alarming power of political correctness. 'Élitism' is used to decry quality; to make people think that pop music is the equivalent of Mozart and soap opera of Shakespeare. No encouragement is needed to listen to pop music or watch soap opera, whereas people might miss out on Mozart and Shakespeare. If it is thought that this would not matter, we are indeed on a slippery slope to nowhere. 'Racism' is used only in the context of white attitudes to blacks, and 'sexism' of men's attitude to women; the words would make more sense if they had a two-way application.

I find it surprising that great changes can take place in our society without anyone seeming to foresee the inevitable results. For decades every organization from giant companies to small businesses has never stopped looking for ways in which it could cut its staff. They have invested in every available piece of technology which could replace labour. The inevitable result is massive unemployment: worse, of course, in recession, but always present. We have, quite rightly, become a caring society, so we pay unemployment benefit to those out of work. But some will be jobless for years, some for the rest of their lives. Meanwhile they and their families suffer not only financially but psychologically – as I know well, having been jobless myself when young. Is it not time for serious thought to be given to creating labour-intensive industries, helped by low-interest loans and tax concessions? Such schemes might well cost less than the costs of unemployment benefit and lost taxes – not to mention the hidden costs of illness and family breakdowns.

Most seriously affected are the young who leave school and college for the dole queue. And they could be usefully employed if National Service was reintroduced: not military but community service, and for young women as well as men. I have no doubt that it would change many perceptions – getting young people to see themselves as valued citizens, and making them more employable when their service ended. After the war, colleges greatly preferred students who had completed their National Service, because of the maturity that that experience had given them; and employers would feel the same.

As to single parents, I believe that, however dedicated they may be, the child would develop a richer personality if the missing parent shared in its upbringing. Children often have a natural affinity with one parent – and that could be the one of whom a single-parent child was deprived. Each parent contributes to a child's personality, just as they did to its physique. Of course joint parenting may be impossible; but sometimes women seem actually to make a case for single parenthood. I know that, without my father, I should never have developed those tastes that have brought me the greatest joy.

Words are precious things. They convey not only subtle shades of meaning but stir deep emotions. They enrich our lives when we meet them in our literature. I find it as insensitive to tamper with the writing of the past as it is to retouch a painting or turn a fine building into a bingo hall. The week after my husband died I had to attend the funeral of a friend. I had been spared the pain of his funeral because he had bequeathed his body for anatomical research; but I thought the emotional stress of my friend's funeral would be unbearable. I need not have worried. It was conducted according to the New Prayer Book and the words left me stone-cold. When I hear the argument that people today cannot understand the Book of Common Prayer or the King James's Bible I want to protest that their forbears, with much shorter schooling, had no such difficulty. After writing this I found unexpected support in A.E. Housman's lecture on 'The Name and Nature of Poetry', in which he says, 'Poetry is not the thing said but a way of saying it', and goes on to quote a line of the 49th Psalm from the Book of Common Prayer, saying: 'That is to me so moving that I can hardly keep my voice steady in reading it; and that this is the effect of language I can ascertain by experiment: the same thought in the Bible version I can read without emotion.'

The value of words in everyday life is that they should give a clear description of facts or ideas. Highly developed languages have huge vocabularies, so that there should be a word that captures every nuance. Unfortunately our individual vocabularies grow smaller, and there is a new tendency to dodge accurate words for vague counterparts. People are described as 'terminally ill' when they are dying. Shall we modernize Shakespeare and make Antony tell Cleopatra, 'I am terminally ill, Egypt; terminally ill.'? Those who have been shot, or injured by a bomb, are also described as 'ill', when in fact they are wounded – which is quite a different matter. No one is sacked; they are 'made redundant'. Famine victims will soon be called 'malnourished' rather than starving. The very clarity of words seems to frighten us; but in blurring the word we blur the reality, and so the appropriate reaction.

Though I no longer go to church, I cannot imagine life without Christianity. I revere it for having inspired architecture, art, literature and music of supreme quality, and for being a polestar to steer by. What I find sad is that, although all religions require their followers to act virtuously, they persist in emphasizing differences instead of similarities, and so set people of different faiths against one another. I would welcome an Eco-religion – teaching universal goodwill, while individual faiths keep the rites they cherish.

Believers and agnostics alike could give life a new quality by trying to follow Kant's precept: 'Act in such a way that you could wish it to become universal law.' That catches us all out; for we excuse our wrongdoing by special pleading, giving ourselves the right to do things we would deplore if done by others. Thieves, cheats, liars and muggers would be the last to wish that everyone did the same.

Human beings are animals – so how did we come to lack the praiseworthy instincts possessed by most members of the animal kingdom? Animals and birds place the well-being of their offspring before everything else. They are never too tired to search for food for them; they face dangerous predators to protect them. And animals can subordinate their own desires to the well-being of their group. Some years ago an island in the St Lawrence came under scrutiny. Deer lived on it; there was no access to the mainland; how could that small area support a growing population? The answer was that it did not grow. Mating took place only between the leading male and female. Human development has largely wiped instinct out of our make-up, and it has not been replaced by any other controlling force, such as foresight or even common sense. In general, the human herd seems to be unable to think in a communal way. Only crises, such as war, unite people so powerfully that even their lives are of secondary concern.

It is this inability to relate to a wider society that causes vandalism in tower blocks. For me, living in a mews house was like living in a village; everyone knew one another by sight, if not by name. In a block of flats the occupants rarely exchange a greeting. Town planning and architectural design certainly play a large part in promoting either a communal spirit or alienation – with the consequences which each can bring.

As an almost lifelong socialist, it was painful to me to realize that my belief was based on a delusion: that people will think and act in ways which benefit their community. I, like other socialists, thought that when things became State property everyone would regard them as their own and would treat them accordingly; but vandalism and graffiti are more often done on public than on private property. When my husband drew a Leningrad truck-driver's attention to the bricks being broken by his careless unloading, all he got in reply was the Russian equivalent of 'So what?'

I can think of nothing that contributes more to good performance, at no cost, than praise: yet it is used sparingly in business and personal life. Achievement should be praised, not taken for granted. Once, at *Vogue*, I tackled my boss, saying that, for months, he had made no comment on the magazine issues. He said, surely I knew that he would have complained if there had been something he hadn't liked. 'Not good enough,' I said. Today, 'Let us now praise famous men' is out of fashion. The trend is to pull the famous off their pedestals by digging up unsavoury aspects of their lives, which have no bearing on the quality of creative or other work. Again I find support from A.E. Housman, who said: 'The centre of interest in a poet is his poetry: not his themes, his doctrines, his opinions, his life or conduct.' To redress the balance of heroes pulled off pedestals, some devote themselves to rehabilitating villains, from Judas Iscariot, through Richard III, to Jack the Ripper.

Neither in life nor literature does one often come across that shock of wonder which made Wordsworth write, 'My heart leaps up when I behold a rainbow in the sky.' But I must be careful not to sound like the Scottish aunt who wrote to a contemporary of mine, on her eighteenth birthday, 'I fear that you will never have the zest for life which I had at your age; but if you read the works of Sir Walter Scott and keep your elbows off the table, the rest will follow.' But I must add that this aunt showed her continued zest for life when she invited her niece to go with her to a cocktail party, a twenties' novelty to which neither of them had been before. Told that her aunt wanted lemonade, my friend found a jug of yellow liquid, to be thinned with water. Nearby was just the thing. She topped up the glass – and her aunt, after the first sip, uttered the immortal words, 'If this is lemonade, it is very good lemonade.' The clear liquid was gin; and the aunt was so impressed that she cleared the port and sherry from her sideboard, filled it with gin, and lived happily ever after.

I feel concerned at the lowered age of active sexuality, because children – and that's what many participants are – have no thought of commitment; they are simply trying out a new experience. But having sex is not like taking an untried dish off the fast-food shelf. It can lead to emotional stress which even older people find difficulty in handling. It can also lead to pregnancy, which changes a life that has barely begun.

I think, too, that our existence has to be spaced out. Nature itself seems to do that, sometimes. Men of genius, such as Keats and Schiele, who died in their twenties, and Schubert and Mozart, who died in their thirties, were somehow empowered to pour out a spate of creativity during their short life-span, while others could afford to bring out their work more slowly. In earlier centuries, when life expectancy was short, boys in their teens led armies into battle and were married to still younger girls. When Lady Capulet told Juliet that many girls in Verona, of her age (thought to be early teens), were 'happy mothers', she was speaking in a period when she herself would be unlikely to live beyond her forties. So the whole life experience had to be packed into little more than half the span we can expect now. The ability to give and to feel sexual pleasure is not among the most long-lived of human qualities. All the more reason for its experience not to be frittered away in passing encounters, but to be delayed for a while, till it can help lay the foundation of a more lasting relationship.

When my father was a young radical in the 1890s republicanism was all the rage. I have never understood why it has such an appeal to the Left – surfacing again now – because it seems to forget that the democratic system creates losers as well as winners. It is bad enough to endure government by a party one dislikes without having a head of state of the same ilk. Is it really more democratic to have a political president who is the head of government but never appears in his parliament to face questioning? And, if he is to be simply a figurehead, how does one go about picking candidates from the population? I think a long-term apolitical head of state, representing the whole nation, and taking care of the ceremonial and social duties that clutter the programmes of political presidents, is the best solution; and a constitutional monarchy fills that bill.

Democratic countries are ardent missionaries in the business of selling democracy to the citizens of less enlightened regimes. Yet

I think there should be two warnings on the packet – and they are warnings that the citizens of democratic countries should be aware of, too. The first is that democracy has no real meaning unless citizens play their part, taking an active interest in politics and voting at elections. The other warning is that fear of adverse voting makes governments cowardly; where they should lead, they are apt to follow what they believe to be majority opinion. But we need leaders with the courage to ask for sacrifices, and the ability to persuade us that these are necessary. When we respond to a charity appeal, we willingly forgo the pleasure of spending money in our own way, because we have been convinced of the importance of that cause. There are many good causes in the public sector, and their claim should be forcibly put to us. 'Where there is no vision the people perish.' We need leaders with vision; and we must give them confidence that we can share that vision.

Epilogue

After Victor died it would have been my instinct to find some voluntary work to occupy me. But there was soon to be another disaster: my sister was knocked down by a car while staying with me and was in hospital for six months. I soon realized that she was leaving her food untouched, simply drinking cups of tea, and going out like a light. I asked to see a dietician, who had nothing to suggest but Complan; light food, suitable for invalids, was not on the menu in her mind any more than it was in actuality. The patient in the neighbouring bed described their large helpings of meat and vegetables as 'suitable for Boy Scouts on a camping holiday' – and this in a ward of patients not only bedridden but mostly of an age when only light meals would be eaten, even if they were active at home.

The ward sister gave me permission to bring in snacks and heat them up on the hotplate in the ward 'kitchen', where meals were not cooked but served. This I did twice a day – at first forcing the spoon between my sister's clenched teeth. (A nurse commented, 'We should be doing this.') I was careful to get out of the kitchen well before serving time, but the unacceptable aspect of trade-union power was soon manifest. The sister – no longer sovereign in her own domain – told me that the cleaners objected to my using the kitchen and that I was to leave my snacks to be heated up by the staff. The final irony occurred when a fire in the hospital kitchens caused patients to be evacuated to another, much less prestigious, hospital, where there was an alternative to each main course – some light dish like mince or fish, with puréed vegetable. This not only gave many patients the only type of meal they could enjoy, but saved the cost of uneaten platefuls being scraped into the bin. Surely the NHS could give guide-lines on something so obvious.

While I was in this state of frustration and distress, Victor's Hungarian doctor dropped in to see me. He was a remarkable man, who had fled his country in the upheavals of 1957 and whose devoted care had prolonged Victor's life. He listened to my lament and said, 'At least you're needed.' Those words hit me like a revelation. They made me realize how fortunate I was to be needed, while many of my contemporaries were neither needed nor even wanted. My sister's already fading memory was wiped out by the trauma of her experience; and shortly after leaving hospital she chose to enter a home. When I had got her settled I looked for voluntary work, and found it in the membership department of the SDP (Social Democratic Party). Later I voted for the Liberal merger and continued to work with the Liberal Democrats – pulling out a few months before the completion of a ten-year stint, in order to write this book.

Now it is finished, what is there for me to do? I have always needed work: needed it even more than companionship, because I am one of those fortunate people who do not feel lonely when alone. I found it extraordinary that Victor, who had an infinitely more confident character than I, had such a fear of loneliness. Always an early riser, he would be sitting at the breakfast table before I arrived, but without touching food or drink. This was not so much a matter of courtesy as because he hated to eat by himself. He used to say that if I were the first to die, he would kill himself; and this frightened me because, since he was a Russian of his generation, who had fought a duel in his youth, kept pistols in his desk drawer (and tried to teach me how to use them against an intruder), I thought it was likely to be true. Again this would have been through his fear of loneliness.

I no longer feel needed. Yet I hope my life will end before I am not wanted, for then I should be forced to abandon a philosophy formed from a lifetime's experience: that with every gain there is a loss, and with every loss there is a gain. Of course the two may be far from comparable, but I have never known either gain or loss to be total. It is when loss becomes so, that life is no longer worth living.

Who's Who

LASCELLES ABERCROMBIE (1881–1938), poet, lecturer and professor at the Universities of Liverpool, Leeds, London, Cambridge and Oxford. Published numerous volumes of lectures. His literary works include *Thomas Hardy: A Critical Study*, and his volumes of verse *Interludes and Poems* and *Mary and the Bramble*. A play, *The Sale of St Thomas*, appeared in 1911.

SIR MAX BEERBOHM (1872–1956), essayist, caricaturist and legendary wit. Wrote for *The Yellow Book* and succeeded Bernard Shaw as dramatic critic of *The Saturday Review*. His books include *A Christmas Garland*, *Seven Men* and *Zuleika Dobson*.

(ROBERT) LAURENCE BINYON (1869–1943). British Museum career in departments of printed books, and prints and drawings. Keeper of the oriental paintings and prints. Published books on many aspects of art and various volumes of verse. His *Collected Poems* appeared in 1931. His plays include: *Attila*, *Arthur* and *Boadicea*.

GORDON BOTTOMLEY (1874–1948), poet and playwright. His poetry collections include: *The Crier by Night*, *Chambers of Imagery* and *Poems of Thirty Years*; and his plays: *King Lear's Wife*, *Gruach*, *Deirdre* and *Kate Kennedy*.

ROBERT (SEYMOUR) BRIDGES (1844–1930), Poet Laureate and playwright. After studying medicine at St Bartholomew's, worked as casualty physician there and at Great Ormond Street Hospital. Gave up medicine in 1882. His poetry includes *The Growth of Love* and *Eros and Psyche*. His anthology in English and French, *The Spirit of Man*, appeared in 1916 and *New Verse* in 1925. He also wrote eight plays.

(EDWARD HENRY) GORDON CRAIG (1872–1966), actor, actor-manager, stage designer and producer, writer on theatrical subjects such as Henry Irving and Ellen Terry. His considerable influence on modern stage production was conveyed through his books *The Art of the Theatre* (1905), *Towards a New Theatre* (1913) and *Scene* (1923), and his magazine *The Mask*. His autobiography, *Index to the Story of My Days*, was published in 1957.

WALTER (JOHN) DE LA MARE (1873–1956), poet and storyteller. His works include: *The Listeners and Other Poems*, *The Veil and Other Poems*, *Peacock Pie*, *Down-adown-Derry*, the novel *Memoirs of a Midget*, and an anthology of verse and prose for children, *Come Hither*, published in 1923.

JOHN DRINKWATER (1882–1937), poet and playwright, actor and actor-manager. Co-founder of the Pilgrim Players – later the Birmingham Repertory Theatre. Best known for his chronicle plays, which include: *Abraham Lincoln*, *Mary Stuart*, *Oliver Cromwell*, *Robert E. Lee* and *Robert Burns*; while *Bird in Hand* is a comedy. His many books of verse include: *Olton Pools*, *Collected Poems*, *New Poems* and *Summer Harvest*. His autobiographical books, *Inheritance and Discovery* appeared in 1931/3.

OLIVER ELTON (1861–1945), scholar, lecturer in English at Manchester, and from 1900 to 1925 professor of English at Liverpool. His works include: *The Augustan Ages*; *Michael Drayton*; *Surveys of English Literature* (in three volumes); *The English Muse*; and *Essays and Addresses*.

HUGH (I'ANSON) FAUSSET (1895–1965), critic and poet. His studies include: *Keats*; *Tennyson*; *Donne*; *Coleridge*; *Tolstoi*; *Wordsworth*; and *Whitman*. He also published two volumes of poetry as well as the autobiographical *A Modern Prelude* and *Towards Fidelity*, which appeared in 1933 and 1952 respectively.

ROBIN (ERNEST WILLIAM) FLOWER (1881–1946), scholar and poet of Anglo-Irish parentage. In 1906 joined the staff of the British Museum, and from 1929 to 1944 was deputy keeper of manuscripts. Also lecturer at the British Academy, Royal Society of Literature and at the Universities of Boston, Yale and Chicago. His poetry collections include: *Eire*; *Hymenea*; *Monkey Music*; *The Pilgrim's Way*; *Poems and Translations* and *The Western Island*.

JOHN FREEMAN (1880–1929), poet. His collections of verse include: *Memories of Childhood*; *Stone Trees*; *Presage of Victory*; *Poems New and Old*; *The Grove*; *Prince Absalom*; and *Solomon and Balkis*. He also wrote *Portrait of George Moore* and *Herman Melville*, which appeared in 1922 and 1926.

WILFRID (WILSON) GIBSON (1878–1962), poet. His poetry collections include *Thoroughfares* and *Borderlands*, his earlier verse being assembled in *Collected Poems 1905–1925*. Later volumes were *Hazards*, *Islands*, *The Outpost* and *The Island Stag*. He also wrote various plays, including *Womenkind*, *Kestrel Edge* and *Within Four Walls*.

A.E. (ALFRED EDWARD) HOUSMAN (1859–1936), poet and professor of Latin at University College, London, and then at Cambridge, where he was a fellow of Trinity College. Published many papers in *The Classical Review* and *The Classical Quarterly*. His three poetry volumes were: *A Shropshire Lad* (1896); *Last Poems* (1922); and *More Poems* (1936). His book of criticism, *The Nature of Poetry*, appeared in 1933.

ALICE (CHRISTIANA GERTRUDE) MEYNELL (1847–1922), poet and essayist. Her first volume of verse, *Preludes*, was published in 1875. Other volumes followed: *Poems*; *Other Poems*; *Later Poems*; *A Father of Women*; and the posthumous *Last Poems*, which appeared in 1923.

PAUL NASH (1889–1946), artist, designer and writer. Held his first exhibition in 1911. Became an official war artist in 1917 (remembered especially for his poignant *Menin Road*, 1919). For a while taught at the Royal College of Art. In 1939 again became a war artist, for the Air Ministry and Ministry of Information, producing such works as *Battle of Britain* and *Totes Meer*. His autobiography, *Outline*, was published in 1949.

SIR WILLIAM ROTHENSTEIN (1872–1945), artist, principal of the Royal College of Art, 1920–35. Father of (Sir) John (1901–92), director and keeper of the Tate Gallery, 1938–64, and the painter Michael (1908–93).

EMERY WALKER (1851–1933), printer. Helped William Morris establish the Kelmscott Press at Hammersmith. Founded (with Walter Crane) the Arts and Crafts Exhibition Society, and (with Cobden-Sanderson) the Doves Press.

Index